ENLIGHTENMENT
a beginne

LEO GOUGH

A catalogue record for this title is available from The British Library

ISBN 0 340 70515 9

First published 1997
Impression number 10 9 8 7 6 5 4 3 2 1
Year   2002 2001 2000 1999 1998 1997

Typeset by Transet Limited, Coventry, England.
Printed in Great Britain for Hodder & Stoughton Educational, a division of Hodder
Headline Plc, 338 Euston Road, London NW1 3BH by Cox and Wyman Limited,
Reading, Berks.

CONTENTS

INTRODUCTION

Human beings have not changed very much in a very long time: that is to say that although we can see innumerable changes in the outer part of our lives going on all the time – in technology, style of dress, language, lifestyle and so on – inwardly, our drives, feelings and mental capacity have not really changed in thousands of years.

Imagine going back in time to a place where modern technology was absent. How much could you teach them about our world? Could you show them, for instance, how to make a silicon chip, or an internal combustion engine or penicillin? Outside the specialised knowledge of your own particular profession you probably wouldn't be able to do much more than give the ancient people a general description of what is possible in our time. Let's suppose that the place you went back to was somewhere in the Midwest of the USA and the time was 600 years ago. The Native Americans you meet have no horses and have not yet encountered people from the Old World. Let's assume you get to first base with them, learn their language and settle down to live with them. No doubt you could teach them a few useful things, and surely you would also learn useful skills from them too – but even if you lived with them for 40 years, would you have them driving around in cars and using computers?

My point is that the 'outside' world – all the systems and machines and organisations and structures and bodies of knowledge that go to make up society – is beyond the control of any single individual. No one person understands it all or knows how it all works; this is because civilisation develops over centuries and builds on the efforts of generation after generation. As individuals, we are born into the

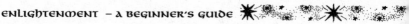

modern world and we know how to get along in it, but we are not masters of it; we didn't create it.

What you would find in common with the Native American tribe of 600 years ago would be your humanity, your human nature – that strange collection of mental and emotional processes that go to make up a person. Your cultures might be different, but, assuming you made friends with them, you would, I suggest, find that they were inwardly not all that different from you: they might be braver, wiser and physically stronger than you because of the life they led, but they, like you, would still be human beings, fated to live for a few decades, to struggle and experience the pains and joys of living and then to disappear from the face of the earth.

There is speculation that many many thousands of years ago people really were inwardly different from how they are now, and that, for instance, their brains were so different that they 'thought' in pictures and saw visions in 3D that seemed to be as vivid and tangible as the objects in the real world. No one knows for certain whether this is true, but even if it were, it does not affect the assertion that for the last few millenia human beings haven't really changed.

This book is about a set of discoveries that have been made again and again by people all over the world throughout history and which have been kept alive mainly by word of mouth, since they cannot properly be learned from books. These discoveries do not relate to external things – the world out there – but to the inner experience of being. Throughout this book I have referred to these discoveries as the 'Enlightenment tradition' for ease of explanation, but you should not think that this tradition is in any way organised. There is not, for instance, an inner circle of initiates who know all the answers and keep all the secrets.

Enlightenment is something that can come to anyone from any background and any part of the world. It is, in its essence, anarchic, and any attempt to formalise or institutionalise it leads away from the point. It is only a tradition in the sense that people who have been touched by it recognise it in one another in rather the same way as two cabinet-makers might recognise and appreciate one another's skill even though they had undergone very different

training. So when you see references to the 'Enlightenment tradition' in this book, please remember that it just means something which one recognises in oneself and others, and is not tied to any particular philosophy or set of beliefs.

This book draws on ideas about 'enlightenment' which originated in India, and I have tried to show that similar ideas have developed independently in the West. They also exist in most, if not all, other cultures, but there was not space in this small book to investigate these fully, so I have concentrated on 'Indian' methods and views. India is unusual in having a very rich and varied 'spiritual' culture which has allowed very ancient ideas and methods to remain alive. The discoveries of 'jivanmuktas' (liberated individuals) who are long dead have been preserved and passed on and we can still benefit from them.

Don't think that this book is about wearing an orange robe and living in the Himalayas, though; whoever you are, and wherever you are, the perennial enlightenment philosophy which is not a philosophy has something of relevance to you, if you are willing to listen.

I hope that Buddhist readers will not be offended by the references to the Buddha and Buddhism herein. I am not a Buddhist, but, for me, Siddhartha Gautama, known as the Buddha, was a man who truly did discover the secret of life and was able to pass on his discoveries to others. I do not believe that he was the only one to do so, but his teachings are widely available so it seemed helpful to talk about him in the book and to devote the final chapter to a brief retelling of his life and works. The Buddha's story is meaningful to me because it illustrates so powerfully how a person can 'get to the bottom' of the problem of existence – "Who am I and what am I doing here?" – by sheer will-power and determination, combined with, in his case, not so many years of special training.

When writing about these matters one can either use a neutral, third-person voice or refer to oneself. I have chosen the latter course, not because I think I am so perfect and wonderful but because I want you to feel that this subject is human, personal and accessible – I don't want you to be like me, but to be as you truly

are, and to encourage you to think about these matters as real and everyday, and not as high-minded sentiments which an ordinary person cannot live up to. Inevitably this approach has coloured the book with my personality and no doubt there are errors and distortions herein. Please forgive them!

If you have any questions about the content of the book, you are welcome to write to me care of the publishers and I will try to answer them briefly.

I would like to thank Tim Hunt and Denny Peat for their help during the writing of this book.

WHAT IS ENLIGHTENMENT?

The enlightenment examined in this book is nothing to do with that eighteenth-century revolution in scientific and philosophical thinking known as 'the Enlightenment'. The enlightenment we will be looking at is a completely different concept altogether.

Enlightenment is very easy to experience and very hard to describe – it is so simple and everyday, in fact, that most of our time we tend to overlook it. It is much easier to say what enlightenment is not, than to define what it is, so later in this chapter there is a list of things which get confused with enlightenment.

First, though, let's make an attempt to grasp the obvious. Ask yourself the following questions, and when you answer them try to do so by focusing on what you see now, rather than on finding the answers in your memory. Here goes:

- Where am I?
- How does my body feel?
- What sounds do I hear?
- What do I see around me?
- What can I smell?

So far, so good – the answers are straightforward, are they not? Here is another set of questions:

- When, exactly, will I die?
- Why do I feel happy sometimes and sad at other times?
- Where was I before I was born?
- Can I name one thing that I can be sure will last for ever?

1

These questions are unanswerable *unless* you start to use your memory and thoughts to devise some sort of hypothesis – but that is not the point of the exercise. The point of the exercise is to realise that, right here and now, without using your clever brain to think up clever answers, you can effectively answer the second set of questions only by saying 'I don't really know'.

Odd, isn't it? And rather like being a child, isn't it?

Here's another question which is often used to point out the obvious – you are not allowed to answer it by giving your name and address:

- Who am I?

You can give a smart answer, like 'I am a collection of molecules', or a religious answer, like 'I am a human soul', but if you do you are using your memory of concepts which you have studied in the past. When I ask myself who I am, and answer in the 'here and now', no answer comes – it is wordless, a kind of feeling, maybe, but then again not really a feeling, exactly. . . . Enlightenment is full of paradoxes!

Some people who are reading this may have 'got it' first time – if you have, welcome to the obvious!

What's the point?

In the preceding exercise, we tried to notice the obvious, so we can try to define enlightenment as just that, noticing the obvious. For most of us, though, this is unsatisfactory because it seems pointless. In this book I will try to indicate some of the ramifications implied by this noticing of the obvious, but first, here is some important information which you may not be aware of.

The idea of enlightenment has been passed on by word of mouth in certain philosophical and spiritual traditions throughout the world for at least 2,500 years – perhaps for much longer. While it is something that people can discover entirely by themselves, it is more usually discovered with the assistance of friends who have noticed it already – in the Orient, where respect for authority and

one's elders is a major cultural feature, enlightenment is generally passed on by teachers to their students, such as in the famous guru–disciple system of India. Actually, almost everything in India is passed on by gurus; if you are a musician, you learn music from a guru, and if you are a transvestite prostitute you learn your mode of living from a guru.

Gurus have got themselves a bad reputation in the West, partly because of the activities of various unscrupulous cult leaders, but more importantly because our Western cultural/intellectual traditions encourage individualism and value individual freedoms very highly. This has produced excellent results – if lots of people can think for themselves and act freely, they can make new discoveries such as penicillin and the combustion engine, develop industries and professions, build bigger cities, reform societies every decade and so on. Our tradition of individualism has enabled us to make Western culture dominate the world. We don't really like people telling us what to do. We have bitter memories of worldly churchmen, religious wars and harsh philosophies which benefited the few while causing misery for the many. We don't want to throw away our hard-won freedom to become the servants of some guy from the Third World wearing a robe – and if some of us do, aren't they really just being immature, running away from their problems?

Once you have tasted enlightenment, you tend to want to share it. And it is much easier for most people to understand it if they have a friend to show them; it certainly can't be learnt from books, and most people are not the types to determinedly try to find out about it on their own. Hence the need for teachers, or, as I prefer to think of them, friends.

For whatever reason, many people are uncomfortable with trying to fathom the meaning of existence by immersing themselves in oriental philosophies, and this is understandable. If, like me, you have an affinity for them, then they are a legitimate field for inquiry, but if you don't feel comfortable with them, don't worry – there are many enlightenment traditions in Western culture too, some religious and some secular. Later in this book we will discuss some of these Western traditions.

But this still hasn't answered the question, 'what's the point of enlightenment?' There are many points, perhaps an infinite number of them, so here are just a few:

- It leads to better health
- It reduces stress
- It helps to make your mind clearer
- It helps to improve your relations with other human beings
- It helps to improve your judgement
- It helps you to find meaning
- It helps you to be creative.

Does this sound just like a list of benefits from some commercial product? You can't have it both ways – if wanting to know the point of enlightenment means that you want to know the benefits, above is a list of benefits which you can check out for yourself. Since people are different, they describe the benefits differently – for me, a great benefit is realising that however horrible things happen to be at the moment, the totality of all existence is as it should be, meaningful, worthwhile and beyond the mind of mortal humans (I don't expect other people to think that is much of a benefit, though!).

Just for the record, here are a few things enlightenment doesn't do:

- It cannot cure death
- It cannot prevent incurable disease
- It cannot stop you suffering sometimes.

SATORI

A Buddhist monk once told a Chinese emperor that enlightenment is 'vast emptiness, nothing holy'. In Zen, a Japanese variant of Buddhism, emphasis is placed on getting *satori*, which could be defined as a sudden glimpse of reality, involving a perfect clarity of mind. This book is about enlightenment as 'satori', rather than ways of making the experience permanent.

The enlightenment state is not usually permanent. Most people get a glimpse of it and then relapse into other mental states. In fact, enlightenment is such a normal state that everyone experiences it from time to time. It is beyond words, but one way of describing it is to say it comes when one's attention is perfectly focused on 'being here now', wherever 'here' and 'now' happen to be.

Most religions and cultures have words for enlightenment – it is the 'grace' of Christianity, for instance, and the 'soul' of soul music. It is no respecter of persons, and comes to people who you might not think 'deserve' it, and eludes others who seem to be very 'deserving' of it.

What enlightenment isn't

Because it is beyond words, people tend to talk about what enlightenment is not:

- It is not omniscience
- It is not being emotionally attached
- It is not dependent on your beliefs
- It is not being superior to other people
- It is not a business
- It is not a club
- It is not being good
- It is not being virtuous
- It is not hard to attain
- It is not the result of many lifetimes of spiritual struggle
- It is not an intellectual thing.

It just is.

NOW IS THE HAPPIEST TIME OF YOUR LIFE

A famous Zen story tells of a man who is chased by a tiger and climbs a rope up a cliff to escape it. As he climbs, he sees two mice above him chewing through the rope, while below the tiger is roaring at him. He notices a beautiful berry growing on a ledge, picks it and eats, enjoying its delicious flavour.

'Now' really is the happiest time of your life, regardless of the past and the future.

The Buddha had some very strange ideas about what 'now' is. It is said that he taught that all things consist of tiny units called *kalapas*, tens of thousands of times smaller than a speck of dust, and that each kalapa lasts for the briefest of moments, there being a trillion of such moments in the wink of an eye. To a modern mind, this sounds remarkably like what we hear about the subatomic particles of quantum physics. What is different, though, is that the Buddha didn't use a massive particle accelerator to discover them – he said that you could train yourself to 'feel' the kalapas appearing and disappearing in a stream all the time.

If you learn to be really still (of which more later) you can start to experience 'now' very deeply; and, to me, at least, it really is as if the universe is born, lives and dies all in a moment, again and again, eternally. When you feel this you see the forms of things not as hard units but more as a flow, a continuum.

Perhaps all this sounds a bit weird. Don't worry, it is not obligatory to experience the foregoing! Let's approach it from another angle.

'Now' is the happiest time of your life because it is the only time you are ever in. We go through life in a long series of 'now's. Our busy minds and feelings often get in the way of noticing this. We may spend a couple of hours worrying about something that has happened, or is going to happen, or might happen, or never can happen, then occupy ourselves with work, or eating, or talking or watching television ... constant mental activity, combined with physical changes brought about by activities of one kind or another. In most people this inner hurly burly rarely stops, and this is the primary cause of not noticing 'now'.

But what if you have a job? Or children to look after? You don't have time to moon about dreaming when you have to keep your life on track, get food on the table and everything else, do you? That's the way it seems to many people. 'I'd like to switch off my mind,' they say, 'but I can't'.

Actually there is no switching off to be done. It is more useful to see the mind as if it were water – it flows, it moves, but it can gradually become still and shining, perfectly reflecting the world around it. When your mind becomes still, you can work, play, look after the children, talk, watch television, argue with your spouse, and all the rest, but still be in the 'now'.

I have a friend who wants to be in the 'now'. He reads all kinds of books about meditation and philosophy, and his mind takes him on a merry dance around these ideas. It doesn't work because you can't think your way into being still – you just have to learn to be still. My friend thinks it is hard to learn to be still, but it is not!

Below is interesting 'now' exercise:

EXERCISE

This technique was invented by an Englishman called Douglas Harding, who is now in his eighties. It uses your normal perceptions to arrive very quickly and directly at the 'now'.

1 Hold out your hand in front of you and point your finger. Look at what you are pointing at, and mentally register what you see.

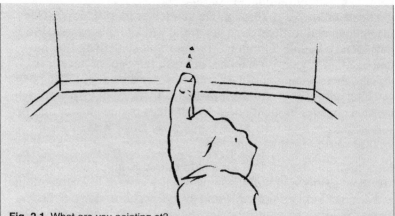

Fig. 2.1 What are you pointing at?

2 Now point at your feet. What are you actually seeing? If it were a photograph, you would say that your feet were towards the top of the frame of the picture, and your chest was at the bottom of the picture – in other words, that as far as your perception is concerned, your body is upside down.

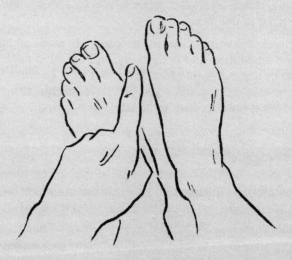

Fig. 2.2 What are you pointing at?

3 Now move your finger so that it points at the parts of your body leading from your feet to your chest, paying close attention to what you are pointing at. This body you are looking at – is it 'you'?

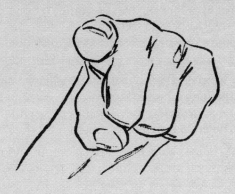

Fig. 2.3 What are you pointing at?

4 Now point directly at your face. You see your finger, but what is it pointing at? What do you see? Can you see what it is pointing at? The honest answer, I suggest, is that you can see nothing.

The 'nothing' explored in the exercise is not exactly an empty nothing, is it? Without using your memory of what you have seen when looking in a mirror, what can you say about it? 'I' am there, am I not?

There's no need to think about it or analyse it – just enjoy the direct, wordless perception of being without 'being' anything in particular. If you can do this, you are in the 'now'.

And, as we have already discussed, 'now' is the happiest time of your life!

Douglas Harding is a beautiful teacher who has built a wonderfully direct methodology for enlightenment around this simple insight. He has been described, lovingly, as a 'spiritual rascal', meaning that he is one who has no need for traditional spiritual institutions (although he respects them and is a learned man).

RENUNCIATION

Now is the happiest time of your life, if you can stay focused in the 'now', but your mind tends to lead your attention away from it. For instance, you may have bad habits, such as smoking and drinking, which make you feel ill and miserable, or worries, or you may get very caught up in your work. One way to reduce the number of things that lead you away from 'nowness' is renunciation.

Renunciation is an extraordinarily unpalatable idea for the modern mind. 'If you want it, go and get it!' – isn't this what we are being told all the time? The idea that it is better to give up something you like (renunciation) than to get as much of it as you can (gratification) goes down like a lead balloon in most quarters.

But it really works. There is something very powerful and mysterious about renunciation. By choosing not to gratify oneself at every opportunity, one becomes strong.

Gandhi used to give up speaking for one day a week. Even if there was an emergency – and for a busy man like Gandhi there often was – he wouldn't speak, but just wrote notes in response.

When you decide to give something up, it often happens that your resolve is immediately tested. Suppose you vow to yourself that you are going to fast all day. Some friends may visit you unexpectedly with some delicious food which they have brought specially for you. 'Oh no,' you think to yourself, 'If only this hadn't happened today of all days. I can't refuse because it will hurt their feelings. I'll eat the food and fast tomorrow instead.' You scoff the food and fail the test.

It really doesn't matter what you decide to give up. The really important thing is to stick to your vow. Start with small vows, like, 'I am going to sit here for the next half an hour, no matter what.' After about five minutes the telephone will ring, or you will suddenly remember an urgent chore, or you will want to urinate – and the test has arrived.

This is what meditation is all about – training the mind to be disciplined and still. You sit and focus your attention on an object, such as your breathing. Fine – for about ten seconds. Then your

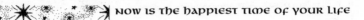

mind begins to wander. You bring your attention back to your breathing. Your mind wanders off again. You bring it back. It wanders off. Off, back, off, back. After a while your mind stops wandering and you stay focused.

Then something else happens. It might be a sudden pain in your body. Or it might be an urgent thought – 'I forgot to pay the telephone bill.' Or it might be a fear, like, 'My son is going to become a heroin addict if he doesn't stop hanging around with those kids who live next door.'

Whatever the content of the distraction, recognise that it is a test of your resolve, and ignore it. Don't fight it, just return your attention to your breathing.

Meditation is the ultimate renunciation. You are renouncing all activity and thoughts for a period, while resolving to stay awake. The mind is not used to this, and doesn't like it; it is habituated to unceasing activity during your waking hours.

If you practise this kind of meditation regularly, you will become able to do it for longer and longer periods. This doesn't mean you have mastered anything, though. The longer you sit, the more subtle and profound the distractions become – agonising pains, strange hallucinations, deeply buried memories, and so on.

Sometimes distractions appear which might be thought of as the 'fruits' of the practice; traditionally they are not discussed in detail in public because they are glamorous and can become addictive, but one can think of them as being special mental abilities which have become awakened through the stilling of the mind.

To illustrate this type of distraction, imagine, for example, that after prolonged practice of meditation you found that your sense of smell was greatly heightened – so much so that it was like being a dog or a cat, being able to perceive a whole history of what had occurred in a place over the past few days simply from minute traces of smells. And suppose that you found that you could use this ability at will. You could walk into an office, say, and know who had been there, whether they had been lying or telling the truth, and the rough gist of what their intentions had been (given that people produce certain

hormones according to their moods and mental states). You might find that you could use this heightened sense of smell in order to make money, since you would have an uncanny ability to 'read' what had occurred in a place recently, and you would be able to conduct business negotiations accordingly. The more successful you became, the more addicted you might become to using the ability until you were neurotically attached to your 'super-smell' sense and the power and money it had brought to you. This is why such 'fruits' are not to be taken too seriously – they are very nice if they appear spontaneously and you don't abuse them, but if you try to control them they will end up controlling you.

Naturally, very few people take good advice, so usually you have to find this out for yourself by going through the whole addiction process and then giving it up – in other words, renouncing it.

Enlightenment does not mean paradise

It often happens to people who join spiritual communities that they find themselves going about with a foolish grin on their faces pretending that everything is wonderful. Indeed, mystics of all traditions have often talked of being spiritually 'drunk' or have likened spiritual life to the ecstasies of falling in love – but they do not mean that life is perfect.

Life plainly is not perfect, and, as far as anyone can tell, it never is going to be perfect. Some religious groups teach that life isn't perfect now, but at some time, in some other place which is not of this world, everyone is going to be happy – or at least, the true believers are. I see no reason to believe them. Let's work with what we know – and what we know, what everyone knows perfectly well, is that life is full of misery and suffering. Not all the time, and not to everyone, but we can be sure that someone, somewhere, is suffering something terrible right now.

We know this, but we have to get on with our lives. Yet in the backs of our minds this awful knowledge of horror remains – I may be living in a palace surrounded by great food and wonderful lovers, but I will know, if I dare to think about it, that somewhere someone has nowhere to live, someone is starving, and someone else is unloved and unwanted.

Not long ago I was walking in a street in Madras, in India, and saw a teenage boy in rags, picking over a huge garbage heap looking for scraps of food. His body was clearly visible through the rags, and, awful to see, his arms and legs were just bones. He looked exactly like one of the prisoners in the pictures of Nazi concentration camps which so haunt us in the West. People react differently when confronted with such realities, but in general the instinct is to try to make sense of it – to build up a net of words and ideas which help us to feel that it's okay to be me even though that person over there is suffering. And, like Mother Theresa, it is sensible to be practical – if you are going to try to help to alleviate gross suffering, you'll be more effective if you set up some kind of establishment which focuses on helping particular kinds of people in a particular way.

Let's leave the practical issues aside for now, though, and concentrate on that tendency to be 'spiritual' by wandering around pretending everything is wonderful. This isn't the enlightenment state; it's just a phase, a mood. Enlightenment is to do with facing reality, in all its horror as well as all its glory. There is no need to develop a body of ideas to 'explain' reality, and no such theory will ever be adequate. All you have to do is to face reality as it comes, seeing it as it is, and responding as you can.

Another thing I have noticed about genuine spiritual communities is that life there is often pretty tough and pretty scary – they aren't a kind of 'Club Enlightenment' where you go for a holiday!

Affirmations

Like renunciation, affirmation is a powerful tool. It can be misused, like anything which is really effective. Educated people often react

badly to affirmations because it seems so stupid to repeat the same thing over and over again, but repetition is the way to 'talk' to deep parts of your mind – those parts which are sometimes called the 'unconscious'.

Here are three positive affirmations:

Now is the happiest time of your life
Now is the happiest time of your life
Now is the happiest time of your life

May all beings be happy.

May all beings realise enlightenment.

IF YOU SEE BUDDHA ON THE ROAD, KILL HIM

This famous Zen saying means that in the end, focusing on a person, living or dead, or an idealised image, such as God or a god, gets in the way of enlightenment. However pure and good the person may have been this still applies. The same goes for any belief system, ideology, or intellectual method; in the end, you have to let them go.

Traditionally, there are many paths to the same goal of enlightenment, and who is to say that new ones cannot be invented? Since there are different types of people, it seems reasonable to think that there might be methods that suit some types of people more than others, and in practice I have found this to be so. Here's one way of categorising the many different paths:

• **Work** Simply doing good, saving lives, caring for the sick and old, protecting the weak, and so on, can lead to enlightenment if you do it with a clear mind and heart. By doing the work you can come to see yourself as you really are, warts and all, and to feel your intimate connection with the rest of existence. Much depends on watching your intentions closely – it is easy to become a professional 'carer' who is full up with self-regard and career ambitions – or a masochist who gets kicks out of their own and other people's misery. And by 'work', I don't just mean charitable works; all useful work that does good and doesn't cause harm can lead to enlightenment, whether it is producing food, doing accounts, writing books, selling things, making things, transporting things, teaching, learning or any other occupation that helps to make the world go round.

- **Energy work**   A whole panoply of 'body work' arts are served up in the West under the New Age umbrella. Many of them are genuine at root. Hatha Yoga, T'ai Chi, Kung Fu and Qi Gong, for instance, are much, much more than simply having some fun once a week. It takes years to make real progress, and you have to be dedicated. Some people are against these arts because they say that they make you vain about your body, but this isn't necessarily so – a person can start feeling vain whatever he or she does. To fully perceive the whole of the universe as a dance, and to participate fully in the dancing, to celebrate the joy of your body and to understand its true nature is not vanity!

- **Thought**   This book is part of this particular way; we are fortunate enough to have wonderful intellects, better, as far as we know, than those of any other kind of sentient being, so why not use them constructively? To ponder and to learn, to think originally and from first principles are wonderful things to do with your mind. In the end, you must let your mind go, perceiving its nature without being caught up in it, and seeing clearly 'who' it is who is thinking. Greek philosophers like Heraclitus and Socrates were brave explorers of the mind, asking silly questions to get sensible answers and looking for the truth with a wonderfully innocent clarity.

- **Love**   There are so many kinds of love and so many ways of giving; people with strong willpower and emotions often find that the best way to 'get out of themselves' is by devoted love of others. Love is a primal force in creation; pure being is pure love. Love is never deluded – it sees things as they really are, and keeps on loving.

- **Upholding a tradition**   What we normally think of as religious observance is part of this path, as is any philosophy, profession or ideology of living. They have a history, a social agenda, a body of knowledge, policies on every material and psychological issue that can affect human beings, and a well-structured system of beliefs and actions to be performed. Voice, words, chanting and praying are part of this path – and whether you are a rabbi or a

Brahmin, a Marxist or a physician, on this path you are part of a hierarchy, having a defined position in it and acknowledging higher authorities in your organisation. Some people find that they make progress only when they are part of some organisation or movement, so if you are one of them, keep at it!

- **Intuitive** This is the realm of spiritual feeling and psychic adventures. Much activity going by the name of meditation lies here (including the 'absorption states', see pages 60–3). On the intuitive path you are a loner, in that you don't connect very well with organised groups, but you feel in touch with all people, all beings, all created things. You are a 'lily of the field' (see page 30), following your intuition, ever conscious of the oneness of all things.

- **Archetypal** This the realm of creativity – not the petty, self-serving creativity of advertising agencies and novelists, but the art of looking into the nature of things to see how they come into being. Not everybody can grasp what this is about; but if you are attracted to Tantra, Tibetan yoga, magic, or ancient Egyptian religion, for instance, then it may be the right path for you. To experience the world as if it is sitting in the palm of your hand, to understand and directly experience what the ancient world meant by the 'gods' is to be travelling on this path.

The foregoing model is based on an interpretation of a number of ancient occult ideas which I encountered in my teens. According to this interpretation, the famous Hindu chakra system, the 'tree of life' in Jewish mysticism, the zodiac, the tarot and many other mystical templates for explaining the universe all reflect one all-encompassing pattern which can be found in any part of it, large or small. I have given up using it because I feel that, while it may possibly be true that there is some vast universal model into which everything fits, constantly trying to make sense of the world by intellectually fitting things into such a construction actually prevents you from seeing things as they are. It became a barrier for me, so I stopped thinking about it – to paraphrase the title of this chapter, I met the chakra system on the road and killed it.

Fig. 3.1 Where does it all end?

KILL KNOWLEDGE?

Most people reading this book will probably have a different kind of 'Buddha' to kill, namely, the 'Buddha' of secular ideology, as taught in schools and universities throughout the West. The better educated you are, the more entrenched are the preconceived attitudes about the world which you have imbibed during your education and which you probably now use in your work. To put it another way, we are all products of our training. Our education twists us, preventing us from having an immediate, unfiltered experience of the world. A criminal lawyer sees the world in one way, a scientist in another, an historian in another, a politician in another, an economist in another, and so on. The immense practical success of Western learning makes it hard to argue with, since one can always think – 'Who is rich? The educated. Who has the widest experience? The educated. Who has the most opportunity? The educated.'

The structure of our societies is built upon education. The uneducated are generally at the bottom, and the educated are generally at the top. It is no coincidence that the majority of individuals in big-time politics are lawyers, for instance. It is hard to

get a well-paid job without educational qualifications, and many people from humble backgrounds struggle desperately to give themselves, or their children, the chance of an education which will, in theory, help them to prosper. Going through the educative progress, these facts are drummed into us, and every year at the best universities several young people commit suicide around the time of the final exams, so miserable are they about their prospects.

When I was studying for university entrance I had an English Literature teacher who had recently obtained an excellent degree from Oxford University (a 'double first'). He was clever, but it hadn't made him happy. For the first time, he was outside the educational system in which he had excelled, and things weren't going well. He was writing a novel based on the Anglo-Saxon poem *Beowulf*, and when the novel was rejected, he killed himself – it was just too painful to realise that commerce (sneered at by English academics) does not work in the same way as passing exams.

This is not to suggest that there is no place for learning, nor that academics are all wrong – my own father was an academic who loved his work and was able to integrate his intellectual learning with a non-intellectual wisdom about life. My point is really that scholars overstep their competence if they arrogantly dismiss the experiences of mystics and say that such things have no validity – it is cultural prejudice rather than objectivity that causes them to do this.

In the Orient, on the other hand, it is common for mystics to say to educated Westerners, 'What good does your knowledge do for you?' We are supposed to nod our heads wisely and agree that it hasn't done us any good, but a legitimate, if nasty, response to such a question might be, 'Well, it helps me to prosper within my society, statistically it gives me a much longer life expectancy than you, you miserable Third World person, it enables me to do more, travel more, know more, get richer, speak more languages and have a broader understanding of the world than you ever will, sitting in the back of beyond, getting brain damage from malnutrition. What's more, my knowledge is enjoyable.'

It would be wrong to suggest that all kinds of education have the same effect. We live in an era of specialisation, and we all know that

no one individual can hope to have more than the sketchiest overview of all the fields of learning now available. This should be a source of wonder, not misery!

To 'kill' the holy cow of knowledge, you have to recognise that thinking all your waking hours stops you from experiencing the 'now'. By all means go on learning and thinking – just don't do it all the time. Set aside a period each day when you don't 'do' anything, and let the mind settle.

Kill drug abuse

Society should grow up in its attitude to drug abuse; it has been around for ever, and it always will be. No amount of legislation, therapy or persecution of victims will put an end to it.

In my experience, many people who take drugs are remarkably nice, talented people; they are not the depraved monsters that the media sometimes depict. Nevertheless, most kinds of drug abuse undoubtedly destroy the user eventually.

Many people take drugs to obtain mystical/'alternative reality' experiences. Modern life can be so horrible that many people feel that the only way to get out of their everyday minds is through drug use. This is particularly the case with users of psychedelics and so-called 'entheogens' (producers of the God within); they produce very intense experiences of a wide variety, often culminating in powerful revelations. If you have experienced these visions, you can only laugh at non-users who say that they are not real. In my view, anyway, there is nothing unreal about these experiences. The trouble with them is threefold:

1 They don't really make you a better person. After the effects have worn off, you are the same as you were. Their power tends to make you feel that the only way to 'get back' to a 'higher reality' is by taking the drug again, and many people end up living sordid everyday lives interspersed with occasional psychedelic adventures.

2 They definitely take a physical toll on your brain and nervous system. People who use psychedelics regularly often display symptoms of neurological dysfunction – halting, disconnected speech, poor short-term memory, mental confusion and an inability to cope with daily life are typical. Most people who start to suffer such symptoms stop taking psychedelics and begin to recover, but some just go on and on. As one hippie friend remarked to me, 'All the really heavy users I knew in the sixties have been wiped off the face of the earth.'

3 They aren't necessary! Using them repeatedly is like being shown an open door again and again, but never being able to go through it. Most of the experiences people have under their influence (for example, visions of the cosmos, visions of the internal workings of the body, astral projection, seeing auras, telepathy, the world of archetypes, clairvoyant perception of earth energies, and greatly improved mental abilities) are obtainable in a healthier and more useful way by the steady practice of occult and spiritual disciplines.

Much more importantly – since these 'hidden' worlds can be as futile as the everyday one – the experiences people have while under the influence of psychedelics of the ultimate source of all realities are attainable without the use of any artificial prop. So give them up before they give you up!

No doubt the foregoing will please no one. People who don't take drugs will say that it is dangerous nonsense, while people who do will say that I am making value judgements. Never mind – perhaps someone will find it useful.

Drugs which are apparently less harmful in moderation, like alcohol and marijuana, whether or not they are socially sanctioned, don't do you much good either. There's no need to be neurotic about it – the occasional drink or joint is not going to kill you – but they stop your mind from working properly, and prevent you, while under the influence, from attaining the enlightenment state. They take their toll on the body and should generally be avoided.

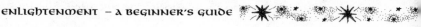

Self-Reliance

Without self-reliance, there can be no enlightenment, because enlightenment is so personal. To non-religious people the importance of self-reliance is often obvious; if you have had the independence of mind to decide, 'There is no God', or 'I have no way of knowing all the answers about existence', then you presumably appreciate the advantages of thinking for yourself.

For many religious people, however, as well as for people who strongly believe in a materialistic ideology, such as Marxism, the idea of self-reliance, particularly the kind which arises from the desire to retain one's own independence in all decisions, creates a lot of difficulty. The problem is that any great ideological movement, religious or secular, deals with social reform. They lay down a system for living which their followers are expected to pursue obediently. To a Christian, for instance, Oriental ideas about enlightenment are dangerous because they are 'antinomian', which is the idea that you don't have to follow a prescribed moral code if you are to experience enlightenment.

The enlightenment tradition does not deal with social issues – it doesn't tell you how other people ought to behave or give you a set of answers for you to apply to the problems of society. Such rules do exist in Buddhism in so far as it has become a religion rather than an exploration of consciousness and existence, but this is, I think, because of the natural tendency of human beings to ruin good things!

From the point of view of the enlightenment tradition, belief systems may often start out well – an inspired leader appears with a disinterested wish to better the lot of humanity, and brings new hope into the lives of the people around him or her. After the leader dies the followers start to make a mess of things, and by the time a few centuries have passed what had originally been an inspired movement has become just another institution, often socially oppressive, and in any case weighed down with rules and customs.

If you don't reclaim your own inner authority and resolve to make your own decisions, you end up doing and thinking as someone else

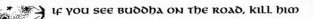

tells you. There are so many forces which want to influence us in one way or another. The government wants us to think certain things and do certain things, as do businesses and many other organisations. This is because to get power in this world you have to be able to influence people, in their thoughts as well as in their behaviour.

Enlightenment isn't about getting power. It is about seeing things as they really are. You can't see things as they really are if you obediently think what other people want you to think. Thus, another Buddha to kill is the Buddha of obedience!

May all beings be happy!

4

GOOD AND EVIL

In Chapter 3 I suggested that disobedience is a prerequisite for enlightenment. This doesn't mean, though, that disobedience is a virtue in itself – otherwise, every immature person who never grew up, every psychopath and every anti-authoritarian radical who is at loggerheads with the state would be experiencing enlightenment. Merely being disobedient doesn't make you wiser or better than those whom you are disobeying. By cutting loose from the bonds that others have put on you, you are faced with new responsibilities – you have to take more responsibility for your own actions and make your own moral choices.

Making moral choices implies some way of distinguishing between 'good' and 'evil'. These are entirely human notions. So far as we know, other animals don't distinguish between good and evil. One might say that other animals are entirely good, since they behave according to their natures; for instance, one can't really say that a predatory animal who kills is 'evil', even if, like mink, they kill much more than they can eat, apparently from the sheer joy of killing. Some animals may appear 'evil' to us because they are dangerous or because they appear to inflict unnecessary suffering on their victims, but we are asking too much of them if we judge them in this way – an animal just does what it does.

Of all the conscious beings that we know of, humans are the only ones self-conscious enough to be aware of chains of cause and effect that reach from far into the past and extend far into the future. Clearly some animals do perceive cause and effect to some degree, but human beings can see more than they can. Perhaps this is all due to the size of our brains.

Amongst human beings themselves, some are much better than others at perceiving chains of cause and effect. Some petty criminals, for instance, seem unable to perceive the inevitable consequences of their actions which to most people appear obvious, and are doomed to keep on repeating the same mistakes. All of us, though, are better at understanding the chains of cause and effect that we know well rather than those that occur to people and in places that are far away. For instance, people who live in Western countries are better at judging the actions of their own kind than they are at judging the actions of people in Muslim countries, who are operating in different circumstances and within a different culture.

For some, 'good' and 'evil' are simply those things which the people around generally accept to be good and evil – to this way of thinking, if it can be called thinking, all child abusers are evil, for example, and all people working in the caring professions are good. More thoughtful people don't accept this, and say that there are no absolutes – everything is a shade of grey, and no person is completely good or completely evil. It isn't really necessary, however, to make any such generalisation; if you are in the 'now', you just take everything on a case-by-case basis.

I have used the slightly unusual phrase 'the chain of cause and effect' because I think this offers a clue to understanding why human beings are so inclined to label things as good or evil. There is never any end to cause and effect. If you pick up a glass and drop it on the floor, you might say that is all there is to it – you pick up the glass and drop it (the cause) and it breaks on the floor (the effect), but in reality there has been an endless chain of events that has led up to the cause (for example, you had to be born, your parents had to be born, human beings had to evolve from other animal forms, oxygen and water had to appear on earth, the solar system had to appear, and so on) and there will be an endless chain of events that follow the effect (for example, there will be broken glass on the floor, someone may clean it up, the glass may go into the garbage, the garbage may be recycled or buried in the earth, the molecules may eventually break down and become part of other things, and so on). It may seem a little ridiculous to look at such a simple event in this way, but this is the way that many oriental sages have looked upon

all events. In fact, there is a type of meditation where you contemplate a simple event and carefully trace the chain of cause and effect of which the event is part, back into the past and forwards into the future. When your mind is very calm and still you can see far more of this chain than you can in your normal everyday state of mind.

EXERCISE

It takes a lot of mental training for most people to get to the point where they can contemplate cause-and-effect chains at will – although most of us occasionally have moments when we see the implications of things very clearly. Here is a basic exercise which, if you practise it regularly, will improve your ability to do so.

Every night, as you lie in bed, send yourself to sleep by practising the following:

1 In your mind's eye, recall the events of the day in reverse order, starting with what you did in the half-hour before going to bed.

2 Next, recall what you did in the half-hour before that, and so on backwards until you remember waking up in the morning.

3 By doing this, you are in effect going backwards and forwards in chunks – you start by remembering the previous half-hour and unrolling it forwards in time, and then jump back to the previous chunk of time and unroll that forwards. This may be difficult at first, but with practice it becomes easy.

4 Once you get to the point of being able to recall the day's events with ease, try recalling them in even more detail – every movement, every word spoken can be recalled with practice.

5 Another approach is to recall not only the day's events, but those of previous days, weeks, months and years so that you run backwards over your life to your birth.

6 Don't make the exercise into a big struggle. It is okay to fall asleep, or to find yourself in a dreamy state where extraneous things come into your mind. If you keep doing the exercise regularly, your mind will start to help you to remember in ways you wouldn't expect.

Fig. 4.1 Which came first? What came before either of them? What came before that? And what came before that? . . .

Karma

Observing the chain of cause and effect is how the idea of 'karma' was conceived. Karma is a much misunderstood notion in the West – and in the East, too! Karma doesn't really offer a simple explanation of everything – it doesn't, for instance, really mean that if you are bad in your life you will be reborn as an animal. Karma is just a way of describing the immensely complex and ultimately incomprehensible interaction of causes and effects in the world and within ourselves. As human beings we can perceive only a small part of this chain with any clarity, and in order to be practical we have to use rules of thumb – working hypotheses – in order to make judgements and carry on with our lives.

This is where moral codes come in – everyone has some kind of code, personal to them, which they use to come to decisions in daily life. A man's code might, for example, include the idea that hitting his girlfriend is wrong even if he would like to hit her. This is a useful rule of thumb, since he can't sit down and think through all the consequences of his actions every time he feels moved to do something. Occasionally, he might think about it and talk about it to

other people, but most of the time he just keeps that little rule in his head. How did it get there? Perhaps it got there just because his parents and teachers taught him not to hit people. Perhaps it got there because he knew a woman who suffered greatly because her boyfriend hit her. Or perhaps in the past he hit a girlfriend and learned to regret doing so. If you think about it carefully, you can see that all society's rules develop over a long time and are moulded and shaped by human behaviour and experiences in an immensely complicated way.

Since morality is so complex and ambiguous, many people become frightened of thinking too deeply about it. Someone who is better at arguing than you might be able to defeat you in a dispute, and this worries people so much that they look for easy answers. It takes strength of mind to appreciate that while you might be right about a certain issue, there may be others who will never agree with you and that you may not be able to come to any understanding with them. For this reason, the traditional advice has always been to refrain from talking too much with other people about your own moral sensibilities. There are many people in this world who take a malicious pleasure in playing with other people's minds.

A Brazilian friend of mine has a great phrase for dealing with this kind of mental aggression. She says to herself, 'Do they put food on my table?' In her case, the answer is always 'No' because she makes a point of being completely self-reliant. For her, the fact that other people don't feed her reminds her that she doesn't need them in order to survive.

While I do think that you can cultivate sensitivity to such an extent that you can really see into other people's inner worlds, those of us who cannot do so are well served by ignoring other people's views to a large degree. You are the one who has to deal with your own life, to feed and clothe yourself and protect yourself from harm, so don't pay too much attention to what other people think you ought to be doing. Remind yourself that you, and you alone, are responsible for your own life, and ask yourself, 'Do they put bread on my table?'

But what if it's your boss who is abusing you? Your boss is the person who puts bread on your table. In this case, you can remind

yourself that while you may love your company or whatever organisation you work for, it doesn't love you back. Ultimately you will be on your own when you retire, so don't be too afraid of facing your 'aloneness' right now. Employers often use the fear of getting fired to manipulate their employees. Be brave and don't let them do this to you.

The value of life

Life is an extraordinary, wonderful thing. As far as we can tell from the world around us, only living things can be conscious. Given that living is sweet, not only to us humans but also to animals and in a weird way to plants too, as any real gardener knows, it is a real shame to take it away. It gets taken away soon enough. These sentiments are behind the vegetarianism of the Hindus and the anti-killing ethos of the modern world.

The Jains, a religious group that began in India at the same time as Buddhism, have taken this idea in an extraordinary direction; Jain holy men wear veils so that they do not accidentally inhale some small insect and kill it, and sweep the ground ahead of them as they walk so that they don't accidentally tread on any living creature. While I applaud the impulse to do this, it does seem rather impractical! Also, biology shows us that there are many microscopic living beings which are killing and being killed within us and without us all the time, so we actually have no hope of completely refraining from killing any living creature.

Like other animals, sometimes we must kill in order to protect our own or other people's lives. Although this is rare in our so-called civilised societies, these situations do arise. Recently, someone I know was stabbed to death while on holiday in Guatemala for the money he had in his pocket. If he had been able to save himself by killing the robber, I doubt if many people would have thought any the worse of him.

Killing rarely happens in the way it is portrayed in the movies, though – it is unusual to be so clear cut. Although I have been

fortunate in never having killed a human being, I have seen a person killed and know people who have killed in war. 'Men like war, and women like warriors', so the saying goes, and it is clear that human beings of both sexes are perfectly capable of killing their own kind – like other animals, we are natural killers. In an atmosphere of violence most people seem to 'click in' to an aggressive survival mode very easily.

There is much that can be said about killing, but nothing focuses your mind so clearly as experiencing it directly, whether as a participant or as an observer. If this has happened to you, you don't feel very inclined to lay down the law about it except, perhaps, to say that it is desperately wasteful and sad – and another little rule is added to the moral code in your head!

From the point of view of the enlightenment tradition, this famous saying of Jesus expresses the exquisite beauty and value of life:

> *Consider the lilies of the field, how they grow; they toil not, neither do they spin:*
>
> *And yet I say unto you, that even Solomon in all his glory was not arrayed like one of these.*

Matthew 6:28

How our behaviour changes when we are desperate

When life is going along peacefully and we are happily doing what we have to do, it is easy to dream up all kinds of generalities about right and wrong. When the going gets tough, we have to throw out many of these ideas. Here's a Zen story that illustrates this.

In a time of war and plague, a man became so hungry that he decided to become a robber. Going out to the city gates, he saw a woman cutting the hair from a corpse to sell it for food. Approaching her, he asked her what she was doing. She explained that she was so hungry that she felt forced to do this horrible thing. The man then robbed her of her clothes, explaining that he, too, was the victim of necessity.

The moral of the story is that people sometimes do bad things because they are desperate. One could argue that it is more acceptable to do something bad in times of necessity than when you don't really need to. It would be preferable to be consistent, but no one can say for sure how they would behave if they were put to an extreme test. How would you judge, for example, the many well-to-do bourgeois families who were reduced to prostitution and theft in Beirut during the destruction of Lebanon? When you are fighting for survival, your values and priorities change.

Loving kindness

In the enlightenment tradition, we don't worry too much about setting out a moral code that can be applied to all situations; to do so is rather like law making – you make a rule that seems to work, and then a new situation arises that proves it to be ridiculous so you have to conceive a new rule. Doing what you sincerely feel to be right at the time, and being willing to revise your ideas, is a practical approach to this matter.

There is something you can do, though, that is very beneficial not only to yourself but to the rest of the world, too. This is the practice of 'loving kindness', known to Buddhists as *metta*. Metta has a mysterious transforming power over the mind. The exercise below demonstrates one way of awakening it.

exercise

1 Sit comfortably with your back straight.
2 Let your mind settle by controlling the natural rhythm of your breathing.
3 Think of yourself. Send yourself warm, loving feelings. Wish yourself the best in all aspects of your life. Really feel kind and loving towards yourself. Accept yourself as you are, warts and all, and love yourself.

4 Think of someone you truly love. Normally people are asked to think of their mothers, but if by chance you do not love your mother, think of someone else who you do love, completely and unselfishly. Wish that person the best in all aspects of his or her life. Hold this person in your mind's eye, and feel kind and loving towards him or her.

5 Think of the people who are physically nearby, and send out the same feelings of loving kindness.

6 Think of the whole area you live in, and send out the same feelings of loving kindness to everyone who lives there.

7 Think of the whole country where you live, and send out the same feelings to all people and animals and plants there.

8 Think of the whole region of the world in which you live and send out the same feelings to all people and animals and plants there.

9 Think of the whole world and send out the same feelings to all people and animals and plants that exist in the world.

10 Think of the solar system and send out the same feelings to every corner of it, to every bit of empty space, piece of rock and molecule of gas in it.

11 Think of the whole of the Milky Way and send out the same feelings to every speck of material, whether animate or inanimate, that exists there.

12 Think of the whole universe and send out the same feelings to every sentient being and every object that exists there.

13 Think of all possible universes that ever have or ever will exist, and send out the same feelings to everything that has ever existed or ever will exist.

14 Return your attention to yourself and wait quietly, concentrating on the rhythm of your breathing.

15 Say out loud, 'May all beings be happy'.

Nobody is perfect. We all do bad things and we all do good things. We all need love anyway.

May all beings be happy.

5 ETERNITY

*Eternity is not something people like to talk about; if you do,
you're liable to be labelled a dreamer. It doesn't seem to be of any
use to ponder such 'imponderables'. 'What has eternity got to do
with my life here and now?' you might ask.*

Eternity has everything to do with the here and now. It's just been
relegated to the sidelines while we focus on work and pleasure
and money and pushing each other around, and all the other things
that are supposed to be more real and more relevant.

But when we relax and take our ease, thoughts of eternity arise
within us. We watch science documentaries on television about the
vastness of the cosmos. We stare into the fire or gaze at the sunset.
We visit the countryside to get away from the rat-race. We watch
movies that paint pictures of other lives, other places and other
worlds. Many of us like to fantasise about aliens, spirits, or being a
spy or a master criminal. We listen to music.

Then on Monday morning it's back to work and 'reality'. Too much
dreaming, we think, is bad for us – it stops us from earning money.

When we were children we wondered at the newness of the world,
and the richness of it and its boundlessness. Now we're grown up
we have stopped considering it altogether, or put it in a special
compartment called 'free time', to be kept apart from the rest of our
lives and confined within certain allotted hours.

Talking about eternity is generally considered to be bad manners. If
you really want to kill a dinner party conversation, try bringing up
the subject. People have to be pretty drunk before they'll respond.

What a shame to make the only time you'll contemplate the infinite a time when you're intoxicated!

There is a science fiction novel called *Stranger in a Strange Land* by Robert Heinlein, which was much beloved by the Flower Power movement in the 1960s. It introduced an interesting verb called 'to grok' (a made-up word). To grok something means to contemplate it, to become utterly absorbed in it, empathising and merging with it, or becoming one with it. Hippies used to talk about the importance of 'grokking'.

Grokking is the stuff of our dreams – contemporary literature and movies are full of stories of merging, becoming one with, transferring one's identity to . . . . something else. Down in our unconscious minds, something is urging us to grok.

If you get lost in the beauty of a sunset you are grokking it. If you watch a televison documentary about the infinity of the cosmos you are grokking it.

It may all sound very sci-fi and silly, but there's nothing new about it. In the East, where everything seems to take an eternity anyway, it is part of the culture to 'grok'. Indians like to say that the English had to invent cricket in order to give themselves a conception of eternity.

Communing with eternity is wordless. It's hygienic, too, for our inner selves – we are refreshed and integrated by it. It heals us. Going to an art gallery, or a place of worship, or into the countryside helps us to 'get there' easily – but actually anything can do it. Just focusing on things as they are, without thinking about anything in particular, does it.

Human beings are not important

They really aren't! Western culture is based on the opposite notion – that human beings are the most important things that exist, that God has a special job for us, and that somehow the whole universe is a special toy for us to play with.

Imagine for a moment that in other places, out there in the vastness of space and time, there are sentient beings of equal intelligence to humans. Perhaps these beings may be even closer to home – perhaps one day it will be proven that dolphins, say, are just as clever as humans. Being as clever as us, these intelligent non-humans would also wonder what they are doing here, what the universe is, what it all means, and all the other existential questions that all belief systems try to answer. The answers which they came up with would be different from ours, perhaps, but they might also have some elements in common with our own.

It's all speculation, of course, and if you were really hard-nosed you might say that it was pointless speculation. So far as we know, we are the only creatures capable of contemplating the meaning of life, so maybe we are right to assume that this makes us particularly important in the great scheme of things.

Somehow I doubt it. We are a bunch of talking animals living on one small planet orbiting one very average star at the butt end of the vast Milky Way, itself only one of an enormous number of other galaxies spread out across unimaginable distances, our whole species' lifespan destined to last only for an infinitesimal fraction of the life of the universe – and, in oriental tradition, that universe itself only one of a never-ending series of universes – can anyone seriously believe that we are the centre of it all?

It is awesome. It is impossible to grasp. It is terrifying. It is ineffable. Reality is bigger than we are, and if we even began to comprehend it fully it would destroy us. To use traditional language, God is terrible.

Personally, I don't have any problem using the word 'God' to mean the same as 'totality', or 'reality'. Some people do, though. Believing that 'God' is an idea dreamed up by human beings, they feel that it is somehow cheating to talk of God, that it is an excuse for sloppy thinking. Other people turn 'God' into an old man with a beard, or a moralist, or any number of notions.

If the 'G' word bothers you, or is too tied up with negative associations, or seems to get in the way of seeing things as they really are, then I'm sure it is okay to abandon the word. But I'm also

sure that it is okay to use 'God' as a synonym for reality, in its broadest, widest sense if you want to do so.

From the point of view of the enlightenment tradition, it really doesn't matter what you call it and it really doesn't matter if you are religious, agnostic or atheist. The fact remains that we all know that reality is bigger than we are. This is scary. Don't run away from it – turn and face it. As one tiny speck in the vast universe to another, I ask you to recognise how really unimportant we human beings are – not meaningless, not pointless, just not important.

According to Indian tradition, the universe has a sound, 'Om', or 'Aum' – three syllables, 'A' , 'U', 'M'. You probably know that it is written thus in Sanskrit:

Fig. 5.1 'Om' in Sanskrit.

The etymology may be spurious, but it is often claimed that 'Amen' and 'Om' are the same word, the great sound of the universe.

May all beings be happy.

May all beings be enlightened.

Amen.

6

DEATH

It is said that other animals do not know that they must die. To the extent that they are unreflective this may be so – and the same applies to people. In modern societies death is institutionalised and shoved away in orderly systems; we don't see it every day. In poor countries you do see it all the time, and this makes people more conscious of the reality of death.

Death is the great equaliser – however rich and clever you are when you are alive, when you die you are just like anyone else. Dying is done alone, even if you are surrounded by loved ones.

EXERCISE

For this exercise, spend a few minutes thinking about what it might be like to die.

1 Try to imagine the dying process. Feel what it might be like for your heart to stop pumping, your brain to shut down, your body to cease working.
2 Imagine what happens to your body after death. If it is cremated, it goes to ashes quickly, burned to almost nothing in a furnace. If it is buried, it rots. The bacteria inside your body, including the friendly bacteria of the stomach which helped you to digest food while you were alive, now start to feed on your flesh.
3 The early stages of rotting are the most horrible because at this time the corpse still resembles what you were when you were

alive, although the body is distorted horribly, producing ghastly colours and smells. The rotting cadaver is actually dangerous to other human beings because of the risk of infection.

4 After a while the belly explodes, and the flesh rots away. The skeleton remains, held together by sinews. It is no longer so terrible to look upon.

5 Eventually the sinews rot, and the skeleton falls apart into a collection of bones.

6 After a long, long time, depending on the immediate environment, the bones break down into molecules which are absorbed into other things, feeding the plants and animals, joining the soil.

That's it! Once you walked upon the earth, and then you didn't and your body dissolved back into the mass of material from which it came.

Is that all there is to it?

From a purely physical point of view, death is final for any living being. Most people cannot accept that death is the end. If we have not experienced the death of loved ones, we can just get on with life and ignore the issue, but as soon as people whom we know and love start dying, as they inevitably will, we have to wonder what it all means.

Bereavement strategies

Before indulging in further speculation about post-mortem existences or the meaning of death, let's look at some of the things that happen to bereaved people.

How we feel about people when they are alive greatly influences our reactions when they die. There are people of whom, when they die, one can legitimately say 'Good riddance'. There are people in this world who are so cruel and do so much harm to those around them

that their deaths are a blessing to others. We are supposed to feel guilty about having such feelings, but I don't see why. I don't mean that it is good to exult at someone's death or to dance on their grave – that's nasty! – but it is hypocritical to pretend that someone was a wonderful person when they weren't. I went to a funeral once where the priest began his address by saying 'X was not a good man. He was a big man.' Everyone in the congregation, including his wife and children, knew that this was true.

Deaths are very varied in the reactions they produce amongst the mourners. There are tragic deaths, pointless deaths, merciful deaths, happy deaths, horrible deaths, unlucky deaths and so on. Many people feel compelled to talk about the deceased, which is healthy in so far as it helps them to reflect on the truth about that person's life, and about the human condition in general.

I think that, for the people who are most affected by the loss of the deceased, it is important to recognise that the process of coming to terms with what has happened is a long one. You shouldn't make any quick decisions – losing someone older than you who featured strongly in your development, such as a parent, has a very powerful effect on your own sense of identity. Once you went through life always knowing that person was there, ready to help and advise you. Now he or she is gone and you are no longer a child – you have to somehow take back the role you had assigned to them, and incorporate it within yourself.

With all our modern neuroses and confusions, the death of parents often gives rise to mixed feelings. We loved them but we also hated them – we fought them or were hurt by them. All these feelings are thrown up forcefully by the death, and there is no longer anyone there to feel resentful towards or to argue with. They have gone and we are left with our feelings unresolved. Be patient and allow the psychological process of digestion to take its course within yourself.

When my mother died, the two people who were closest to her were a cousin and myself. My mother had a massive cerebral haemorrhage and was taken to hospital. I arrived and sat by her bedside, watching her body struggling to breathe as it filled with mucus (she was in her seventies and a heavy smoker), and talking

to her, hoping that perhaps she could hear me. Every so often a nurse would use a tube to pump out the mucus. My aunt telephoned from abroad and I told her my mother was dying. She didn't believe me.

My cousin arrived and I met her in a corridor. Grief had made her angry – she started criticising me for all the things she thought were wrong about my behaviour and feelings towards my mother. I suppose I could have been very offended, but it was plain that she was talking from pain and sorrow, not from any real desire to hurt me.

We sat for hours by the bedside, watching my mother's body struggle to live and gradually get weaker. Finally she died. How did we know? She gave the famous death rattle and stopped breathing. At that point we were drinking mugs of tea. We were silent for a long time. Crude person that I am, I slurped my tea. My cousin was angry at what she thought was disrespect. Disrespectful of her anger, I deliberately slurped again. She got the message and kept quiet. I am recounting this not to say that I behaved properly, but to describe what was going on within me at the time of the death. Somehow, I felt that it was important to remind myself of the 'earthy' part of it all, and my way of doing that was to slurp my tea. Sometimes after a death or a funeral people will go home and frantically make love – to my mind this isn't crazy, but a way of reaffirming the opposites – living and dying, growing and rotting, happy and sad. So don't burden yourself with guilt if you behave oddly when someone dies!

This is a description of one death; not all deaths are like this. After the death comes the funeral, a time when people who knew the deceased come to see the corpse depart officially, as it were. This is a very useful ceremony because death can be so shocking, so earth-shattering, that many people don't really take it in. You may know intellectually that a person has died, but it doesn't seem real. Seeing the coffin lowered into the ground or consumed by the flames is proof that the person has gone – and helps the bereaved realise that it really has happened.

In Italy the corpse is displayed openly during the funeral. In India it is burnt publicly, with a priest or a relative smashing the skull of the

corpse to make sure that it doesn't explode in the flames. It may seem gruesome, but it isn't. It's just another way of making sure that people really see what is going on.

All this is healthy and makes the fact of death easier to bear. When someone dies far away, or in circumstances where there is no ceremonial 'laying to rest', the mourners are often left with unresolved grief for the rest of their lives. That part of the mind that constantly asks 'what if . . .' has no tangible facts to chew on, and so it goes on worrying at the problem.

Many well-meaning people try to tell the bereaved unsubstantiated facts in order to make them feel better. 'He is in heaven now,' for example. How do they know where the person is, or that the person still exists? The short answer is, obviously, that they don't. None of us know.

There is a story of a poor woman who had suffered many disasters and lost many children. When her last baby died, the grief was too much for her. She wandered around, clasping the baby's corpse to her, looking for some miracle worker to bring it back to life. At last she went to the Buddha, so the story goes, and asked him to revive her baby.

Seeing that she was in no condition to be reasoned with, the Buddha said that he would bring the baby back to life if she would bring him some herbs picked in the garden of a house where there had been no death. She went off to look for such a house. She searched for one for a long, long time. Eventually she realised that there was no such place – every household suffers death.

Going back to the Buddha, she finally understood the inevitability of death, and laid the baby's corpse at his feet.

Death and Reality

Death is very real. There is no getting away from it. Whether the circumstances were fair or unfair, whether the deceased had led a full life or was cut off before reaching full potential, whether the

death has caused disaster for others or whether it has been useful, it makes no difference; death is final and there is nothing anyone can do about it. Accepting this, and facing it rather than pushing it into the backs of our minds or covering it up with wish-fulfilling fantasies, we pass through our sorrow.

On 8 June 1972, a little village in Vietnam was bombed with napalm. A girl of nine, Phan Thi Kim Phuc, lost two of her brothers in the attack. Tearing off her blazing clothes, she ran naked down the road past the American soldiers, screaming in fear and pain, and someone took her photograph. The photo won a Pulitzer Prize, and became one of the most famous images of the Vietnam War, helping to turn US public opinion against the conflict.

Kim Phuc is now married with a child and lives in Toronto, Canada. 'I am happy because I'm living without hatred,' she has said. In 1996 she attended a veterans' meeting in Washington DC, and the American soldier who ordered the napalm attack apologised in tears. 'It's alright,' said Kim, 'I forgive, I forgive.'

Life after death?

No one knows what happens after we die. Many of us have a craving for immortality, however, whether by living on through our works or our children, or merely by becoming obsessed with health and fitness. The belief in reincarnation is often a manifestation of the craving for immortality.

Since we know that we don't know what happens after death, why don't we accept the inevitable?

Throughout history the majority of people have always believed in some form of life after death. If you are a tough-minded atheist you may say that this is because people can't accept the fact of annihilation. If you are a credulous spiritualist you may think you have seen some sign that the spirit of one who has died lives on. If you adhere to a religion then you have a doctrine to explain what happens. It is the pain of loss that unites everyone – when you love

someone who dies, a kind of taste of what they were lives on in your memory of them. Eventually, when everyone who knew and loved that person is dead, those memories will go too. A very small number of people will be remembered after that, through visual and written records, but eventually even they will be forgotten.

The Buddhist view of what happens is subtle. Rather than talking of reincarnation, which is the idea that there is a conscious soul that lives on after death and is reborn into other bodies again and again over aeons, they talk about 'rebirth'. The suggestion is that since, as we will see in Chapter 8, there is no essential 'self' anyway, there is nothing to live on in other forms. In this view, rebirth is like ripples on the water, or a candle lighting another candle before it is snuffed out. There is apparent movement but nothing is actually passed on.

To people brought up in Judaeo-Christian culture this concept is weird, since it still suggests that there is some non-physical series of events taking place after death that continues through other earthly lives. In Buddhism it is thought that only very special people who have reached a purified state of mind can really understand the idea of rebirth properly and perceive it for themselves. I am not one of them. For me, the only clue I have that it might be true is my sense that all things are ultimately interconnected and that nothing, whether it is a person, a stone, or the ripples on a wheat field, can really be regarded as being essentially separate from everything else.

If all things that exist are in a continuum, in the way that the colours of the spectrum are a continuum (i.e. there is no specific point at which red becomes orange and blue becomes indigo, etc.) then one can say that there are lines of cause and effect which can be traced from any place or thing (like a human being) in space and time to any other.

This book isn't about trying to become one of those special people who Buddhism talks about. It is simply about enlightenment as 'satori', the occasional glimpses we have of unfiltered reality. To experience satori it is not necessary to know all the answers, or to indulge in endless metaphysical speculation. All that is necessary is to attend to 'now'.

May all beings be happy.

7

BReATbING,
WALKING, SLeepING,
WORKING, pLAYING

*Whatever you are doing, you are already enlightened, in a sense.
There is no mysterious 'Other' to be striven for – it is already right
here, right now, in you and in me. All you have to do is notice it.
It is Being itself.*

To let Being be, you have to stop occupying yourself with trivia.
Silence is important. Lots of silence, lots of just observing what is
happening, is the medicine for noticing your Being. This is hard at
first. Most of us are so habituated to incessant physical and mental
activity that we feel that to stop is laziness. Indeed, it can be just
that; if you are in a torpid state, perhaps because you have a
hangover or because you've eaten too much, then you are not in a
good state of mind to notice your Being. You can notice it anyway in
a torpid state, but for beginners this is the wrong place to start. The
place to start is when you have all the energy and alertness that
would normally make you rush off and do something.

Meditation cannot be learned from a book but only from someone
who has already done it, unless you are one of those extremely rare
people in whom it arises spontaneously in a developed form. In
books one can only read about meditation, which is not the same
thing as doing it. It is a bit like reading a book about how to ride a
bicycle – you can get the general idea, but it doesn't give you the
non-verbal skills you need to keep your balance when you get on a
bike for the first time. The only way to learn to ride a bicycle is by
practice; the only way to learn to swim is by practice; the only way
to learn to play a musical instrument is by practice; and the only
way to learn to meditate is by practice.

So is meditation the same as noticing your Being? Yes and no. As discussed in previous chapters, we all do occasionally notice our own Being without the formal practice of meditation, and, indeed, without necessarily ever having heard of meditation. Meditation can be thought of as a special exercise to make you better at noticing your own Being – thus it isn't the same thing as actually noticing your own Being, in the same way that skipping with a rope isn't the same thing as boxing, even though boxers skip to improve their boxing.

Fig. 7.1

I emphasise this point to make it clear that it is the noticing Being that is important – the 'being in the now' – not the practice of meditation. Many people get into a state of mind where they put 'being in the now' in a little time compartment when they meditate, and ignore 'being in the now' for the rest of their day.

Many people reading this book will have encountered some sort of meditation practice. It exists in all religions, and is encouraged in a rudimentary form in everything from evening yoga classes to martial arts. There is a physical component to it, since we have bodies. Traditionally, emphasis is placed on proper posture and training the body to keep still – hence its association with physical activities. Sadly, meditation is sometimes watered down so much to make it acceptable to students that the point of it is lost. For example, in Hatha Yoga classes some teachers turn meditation into a sort of sing-song, and people go away thinking that meditation is a kind of play-acting at being happy.

Be discriminating about the person you choose to teach you meditation – there are unmistakable signs in a regular meditator that, once you get some experience, you will always be able to recognise. One simple test is to ask yourself how you feel about the person – is he or she an honest, realistic person with an open face, or do you get the feeling that the person is pretending to be something that he or she is not?

Avoiding gullibility

The practice of meditation can lead to all sorts of mental states, none of which are the point of doing it. For instance, many people think that you are supposed to see visions and become blissful. This may happen, but it is not the goal of meditation. The goal of meditation is to see things as they really are, by watching all the things that go on within you and without you. No particular state is considered more or less desirable, although some may be more useful than others.

We'll return to this point later. First, let's examine a phenomenon that has given some organisations teaching meditation a bad name. It's the 'blissing out' phenomenon. When people start meditating and opening themselves up, they sometimes feel full of happiness, a bit like being drunk or high. Unscrupulous people have been known to exploit this, although if you are sincere you will never be seriously damaged by such exploitation – your instincts will protect you. There is nothing wrong with feeling light-headed and happy sometimes, but if you get addicted to it and try to centre your whole life around it, you cease to function effectively in the world – in other words, you are exchanging one partial view of reality for another.

Blissed-out people are extremely gullible. Here's a story that illustrates the problem. Not long ago the Dalai Lama visited Australia and toured various Buddhist communities there. At one place where he stayed the night he left a half-eaten apple in his bedroom. After he had left, the people at the centre were amazed to find that the flesh of the apple hadn't turned brown as it usually does after contact with the air, but had remained a pristine white.

There was great excitement about this and a general sense that some kind of miracle had occurred. People thought that the Dalai Lama was so holy that the apple he had bitten into had somehow defied the normal laws of nature, so they kept it reverently to show to everyone who came to the community. A day or so later a Buddhist friend of mine, who is also a commercial photographer, came to the centre and was proudly shown the apple. He immediately recognised that the apple had been irradiated, a technique used in the food industry to lengthen the shelf-life of food – my friend uses irradiated fruit frequently when photographing because it lasts longer under the hot studio lights.

Irradiated food has a distinctive taste. Evidently the Dalai Lama had bitten into the apple, thought that it was nasty and left it. No miracle had occurred, no supernatural event had taken place – all that had happened was that some people had jumped to the wrong conclusion. We all jump to the wrong conclusions sometimes, but when you are blissed-out all the time you are not using your faculty of discrimination.

Mindfulness

Buddhists call it mindfulness, but it goes by many other names too. You can think of it as paying attention, or 'awareness', or 'awakeness'. The principle is very easy. You simply try to pay close attention to whatever you are doing at the moment.

Suppose you are washing some plates in the kitchen. Instead of thinking about something else, or talking, or listening to the radio, or worrying, focus all your attention on the actual washing of the plates. Look at them, feel them, watch what happens to them and listen to the sounds they make. Be aware of the processes occurring within yourself as you wash them.

Sometimes people say that they always pay attention to what they are doing, not realising that there are times when they do not. Anyone who has progressed a long way in a craft or a profession has developed powerful concentration, but generally this is confined to a narrow band of activities. What is being proposed here is that you remain mindful at all times without driving yourself to do so in the way that we might drive ourselves to read through legal documents or a difficult scientific paper.

I say 'remain mindful' because there is a sense in which it is our natural state to be mindful, although our mental forces are normally scattered. For me, anyway, mindfulness is like coming home.

The more you pay attention to what you are doing, the more you discover. You need 'space' to do this – a kind of slowness, a stillness of the mind. If you fill up your mind with too many things you become scattered and unable to see clearly. For this reason it is a good idea to reduce the amount of unnecessary distractions in your daily life. For example, many people play the radio while they are working and then spend their evenings watching television. Doing this may give you the illusion of relaxation, or may comfort you when you are alone, but it scatters the mind. The incessant chatter of disc jockeys really does weaken your powers of concentration if you listen to them a lot. Television has an even greater power over us. It pumps out constant suggestions to us about what reality is like and how we ought to be. This creates conflict within ourselves. If

you don't believe me, watch how young children are affected by what they see on television. Children take in things and regurgitate them quickly – you can often observe them doing and saying things which they have recently seen on television.

As we get older we learn to filter out the obviously false suggestions from television. If we see television commercials telling us to buy a car, or that a certain brand of washing powder will change our lives, we are usually sceptical about them, but in young children you can often see that they do believe what they see, for a while at least.

Just because we have learned not to believe everything we see and hear in the media doesn't mean that it doesn't affect us. The material goes in anyway, creating subtle distortions of our sense of reality. If you have ever travelled to a poor country and stayed there for a long time you may have noticed the intensity of this assault of information, half-truths and lies on your return home. It is much easier for someone living in simple circumstances, far away from the modern world, to attend to the 'now' than it is for us, because they have fewer distractions.

Fig. 7.2 The daily onslaught

When I was young I lived for a couple of years in a New Age community. A retired Indian army officer, Major Ramchandra, came to stay there. 'Ramji' as we called him, was a delightful old man, small and energetic, always giggling and smiling. He was writing a book about the correspondences between the *Bhagavadgita*, an Indian holy book, and the Gospels. Most of his days were spent in his tiny bedroom, sitting cross-legged on the floor, writing his book. Occasionally I would visit him there. If he ever had anything really important to say he would write it on a piece of paper and hand it to me. Once he handed me a note which read, 'There will be no atom bomb,' meaning that there will be no nuclear war – it was a time when many people, including myself, were afraid that the world was on the brink of destruction.

Ramji was very intuitive. Once we were walking down the street and encountered a young friend of mine who was carrying a folded magazine under his arm.

'What is that you are reading?' asked Ramji, taking the magazine and opening it. It was grossly, richly pornographic. Smiling, Ramji handed it back. My friend and I were embarrassed but Ramji wasn't – it didn't faze him in the least.

This is what enlightened people are like – happy, super-awake and indifferent to the social norms. They attend to what they are doing at all times, free from the internal conflicts which rage within most of us, and have an immense capacity for useful work.

Sex

Human beings seem to be under a compulsion to tell each other how they should behave sexually. Everywhere you look there are strongly held views on what constitutes sexual misconduct, whether masturbation is right or wrong, whether or not homosexuality is 'natural' or 'unnatural' and so on. In the Western world we have supposedly thrown off the sexual oppression of the past and think of ourselves as being remarkably tolerant and allowing great sexual

freedom. This doesn't, however, seem to have lessened the urge in people to tell other people how to run their sex lives.

In the enlightenment tradition we are not particularly interested in telling other people how to run their sex lives, nor are we keen to say that any particular form of sexual behaviour is 'right' or 'wrong'. As dedicated investigators of reality, we watch the appearance and cessation of sexual urges within ourselves without necessarily acting on them.

There is a branch of yoga called 'Tantra', and within Tantra there is a special, rather secret, tradition of sex yoga. It is not for everyone, and it is rare for someone to be initiated into it. In this discipline, and it is a discipline, the sexual acts are investigated deeply, both the inner effects – what is going on inside yourself, and the outer effects – what is going on in the physical world. In the wrong hands it can turn into an excuse for cheap thrills, but for the right people it is a truly profound art.

Unselfish sexual love can be sublime, a reflection on earth of the unceasing appearance and disappearance of created things. Symbolically, it is the 'Chymical Wedding' of the alchemists, the Shiva/Shakti of the yogis, the yab-yum of the Tibetans. It is one of the few things that people do which allows them completely to become one with another person. To some mystics, the whole of the universe is one giant cosmic sexual act. To some people this may seem vulgar; it isn't – it is deep and beautiful.

Personally, I think that people worry far too much about sex. We all practise celibacy, albeit unwillingly, for long periods in our lives. This can make us get carried away when we have the opportunity for sex, and, like all powerful things, it can be dangerous. We can become enslaved to psycho-sexual urges, tormenting ourselves with the pain of losing someone, not having them, or being betrayed by them. All these problems are related to selfishness, or, as it is called in the enlightenment tradition, clinging.

Clinging does not only mean clinging to a person – if there is anything which you cannot bear to give up, which you hope will never end, such as good looks, attractiveness or independence, you

Fig. 7.3 Cosmic union

are clinging to it. Even if you live happily with a partner for decades, one of you will die first and the happiness will end. If you die at the same time, it has ended. This is the nature of things that exist – they have beginnings, middles and ends.

The important thing about sexual love is to allow it to be unselfish – different sexual orientations cannot be important, in my opinion. It is the love, not who you are loving, that matters. People can be very cruel about this, trying to deny the opportunity for sexual love to others for whom they deem it inappropriate for one reason or another. Spare a thought for physically or mentally disadvantaged people, who have a hard time getting what other people regard as a right.

Black or white, gay or straight, disadvantaged or not, some form of sexual activity with another person is the first, most immediate opportunity we have of experiencing union with that which is outside our little selves. How can this be wrong?

Pay attention!

All activities can be meditations – attending fully to what is happening is all there is to it. When you urinate, pay attention. When you defecate, pay attention. When you spend time with others, pay attention. When you are alone, pay attention.

The more you pay attention, the more you start to discover about yourself. A process of change can spontaneously take place, simply because, say, you see that you eat too much chocolate or that you make too many unnecessary phone calls. Through mindfulness you can start to drop useless habits without a huge struggle – when you notice how silly something is, and you are in a calm state of mind, it is easy simply to decide not to do it, this time.

'Useless habits' are those tendencies within us that create trouble and harm for us. I have hundreds of them – perhaps you do, too. Torturing ourselves about how bad and undisciplined we are doesn't help us to give them up. Pretending that they aren't useless doesn't help us give them up. Being cowardly and saying 'Oh, I'm so weak, and life is so hard, I can't do anything about it' doesn't help us to give them up. Be nice to yourself – give yourself the chance to see yourself in all your glory as well as seeing your 'negative' tendencies.

Practising mindfulness will help, but sometimes it is useful to think about the actual effects of different kinds of actions. For example, we all know how we will feel the next day if we drink too much alcohol. If you habitually drink too much alcohol, you have to suppress that knowledge somehow. So, despite my personal aversion to telling others how to conduct their lives, here is a short extract from the *Sigalaka Sutta*, a Buddhist scripture in which the Buddha gives advice to 'householders' (lay people who live ordinary lives) on how to conduct themselves. In spite of its remoteness in time and various oddities due to a difference in culture, it seems remarkably fresh.

> 7   And which are the six ways of wasting one's substance that
> he does not follow? Addiction to strong drink and sloth-producing
> drugs is one way of wasting one's substance, haunting the streets

at unfitting times is one, attending fairs is one, being addicted to gambling is one, keeping bad company is one, habitual idleness is one.

8   There are these six dangers attached to strong drink and sloth-producing drugs: present waste of money, increased quarrelling, liability to sickness, loss of good name, indecent exposure of one's person, and weakening of the intellect.

9   There are these six dangers attached to haunting the streets at unfitting times: one is defenceless and without protection, and so are one's wife and children, and so is one's property; one is suspected of crimes, and false reports are pinned on one, and one encounters all sorts of unpleasantness.

10   There are these six dangers attached to frequenting fairs: [One is always thinking:] 'Where is there dancing? Where is there singing? Where are they playing music? Where are they reciting? Where is there hand-clapping? Where are there drums?'

11   There are these six dangers attached to gambling: the winner makes enemies, the loser bewails his loss, one wastes one's present wealth, one's word is not trusted in the assembly, one is despised by one's friends and companions, one is not in demand for marriage, because a gambler cannot afford to maintain a wife.

12   There are these six dangers attached to keeping bad company: any gambler, any glutton, any drunkard, any cheat, any trickster, any bully is his friend, his companion.

13   There are these six dangers attached to idleness: Thinking: 'It's too cold', one does not work; thinking: 'It's too hot', one does not work; thinking: 'It's too early', one does not work; thinking: 'It's too late', one does not work; thinking: 'I'm too hungry', one does not work; thinking: 'I'm too full', one does not work . . .

> Thus Have I Heard, The Long Discourses of the Buddha,
> transl. Maurice Walshe, Wisdom Publications, 1987

LITTLE ME AND BIG I

'Aham Brahmasmi'
(I am Brahman, a yogic affirmation)

If you have ever encountered any kind of oriental mysticism before, you will have heard a lot about the 'ego', the 'self' and the 'soul', whether they exist or whether they are merely illusions, how they relate or do not relate to the ultimate reality, whether or not the sense of 'I' is truly the ultimate 'I' and so on. It is hard to understand, and what makes it even harder is that in some oriental languages there are precise terms used for discussing existential questions, but in English, as in other European languages, there are no equivalent precise terms – except, perhaps, for German which lends itself well to philosophical thought.

So when you hear someone talking about 'ego' in this context, you don't know whether they are thinking of 'atma', or 'jiva', or any number of other words with specific meanings which have no corresponding word in English. This is a real problem in Buddhism, as well as in Hinduism and in the anarchic enlightenment tradition. It is also a problem in other belief systems and philosophies; to be able to interpret precisely, a modern Western philosopher must know German, and a Christian must know Hebrew and Classical Greek. Incidentally, Jews know that Christians miss an enormous amount in the Old Testament because it is full of humour – all lost in the translation.

This problem of language is no digression. We know that in the ancient world religious and philosophical texts were preserved in dead languages. The further back we go the less we know, but take,

for example, the Hittites, an ancient people living in Asia Minor who were known only from references to them in the Bible (and, later, from ancient Egyptian records) until archaeological discoveries in the late nineteenth and early twentieth centuries uncovered their cities and vast quantities of clay tablets written in a number of languages.

Discoveries at Boghazkoy, in what is now Turkey, revealed an archive dating from about 1200 BC at a site which had then been occupied for about 400 years. The archive contained at least seven languages:

- **Akkadian**, then the language of diplomacy throughout the Middle East. It is a member of the Afro-Asiatic family of languages which includes modern Arabic, Hebrew, ancient Egyptian and Berber.
- **Cuneiform Hittite** ('Cuneiform' refers to the 'wedge-shaped' writing on the tablets and is used to distinguish this kind of Hittite from another kind called 'hieroglyphic Hittite'). Hittite is a member of the Indo-European (or Indo-Hittite) family of languages which includes English, Sanskrit, the Iranian and the Romance languages.
- **Sumerian**, then a dead language which was used for scholarly and religious writing. It is not related to any other known language.
- **Hurrian**, another 'isolated' language unrelated to any other.
- **Luwian**, a language related to Hittite and ancestral to Lycian, both now long dead.
- **Palaic**, a language related to Hittite.
- **Hattic**, a non-Indo-European language about which little is known.

Thus, in 1200 BC the people living in what is now Boghazkoy were in a world where there were living languages, dead languages and languages that were coming into being. The same is true for us today.

What wise people have written in the past in one language may not make much sense to us who speak another and think in another way, and so their wisdom is lost.

Make no mistake about it. Language governs our thinking, not the other way around. One might even say that language is thinking, for

it provides us with the building blocks with which we create our thoughts and ideas – in some senses we create our selves, our personalities, through language.

If you speak any languages other than your mother tongue, you may have noticed how you change mentally when speaking another language. It is easier, say, to be more artistic, or more witty, or more tough, depending on what language you are speaking at the time.

So when we try to understand ourselves and to find within ourselves our 'personality', our 'self', or our 'ego', we must recognise that without language we couldn't formulate the questions. And, because of language, we cannot see the answer.

When we look to tradition for guidance, we encounter barriers because of language. For instance, without knowing any Sanskrit, can you see that:

> *Nantah-prajnyam, na bahis prajnyam, na prajnyana-ghanam, na prajnyam, naaprajnyam.*

might sound rather better when read aloud, and have a more powerful effect on the psyche, than its English translation:

> *Not outside knowledge, not inside knowledge, not knowledge itself, not ignorance.*

These lines from the *Mandukya Upanishad* perfectly express the enlightenment state in their original language, but not so well in translation.

We can't all be scholars who spend our lives pulling languages apart. If we were, civilisation would come to a grinding halt and there would be nothing to eat. In one sense, this is what 'holy' scriptures are for – to encapsulate wisdom in a form to which everyone can have access. Then, over the centuries, the language becomes 'dead' and only scholars can read it, so the scripture no longer does the intended job.

It is, I believe, the problem of the mortality of languages themselves that is the single most important factor lying behind our lack of understanding of who we are.

This chapter is entitled 'Little me and big I'. I am inventing a special use for these very common words because I know of no commonly understood words for what I want to say. It is not the words themselves that are important, but what they mean. By 'little me' I mean all that within a person that is temporary, subject to birth, decay and death, and by 'big I' I mean that which has no beginning, middle and end.

What is it that has no beginning, middle or end? Nothing. How can 'I' be 'nothing'? It can't be adequately explained in words. It can't be chopped up, weighed and measured. It is not annihilation, so one could say that 'I' is not 'nothing' and not a 'thing', but something in between. You see how difficult it is to use language to express it?

Don't drive yourself crazy trying to understand it; it is Being, it is Now, anybody can experience it and everybody experiences it occasionally. 'Big I' is enlightenment. 'Little me' is being a person. As people, we are both 'big I' and 'little me'.

Relax. Breathe. Be here now.

Fig. 8.1 Reality cannot be described fully – it is too big.

It is natural and understandable for Westerners to give up at this point and say that it is all crazy, oriental mysticism that doesn't mean anything. Our languages and culture, though in very ancient times related to some of those of India, have evolved along a different path. We live today in a world built upon the achievements of rationality and science. Rationality and science have become enemies of our past which was – well, let's say 'pre-scientific'.

We have become cut off from the wisdom of our pre-scientific forefathers (and 'foremothers'). Throughout the Middle Ages in Europe people talked of God, and all existential matters were couched in terms of God. If you can't bear the 'G' word then you will have trouble empathising with what our forefathers thought.

You may have the idea that all speculation about 'I' and 'self' belong only to oriental cultures. If you can accept for a moment – as an hypothesis – the idea that the 'God' of our own pre-scientific culture is a word that approximates to the *nirvana* of Buddhism and the *Aham sakshihi* ('I am the eternal witness') of ancient India – we are entering tricky theological waters here – then you can see that Western history is full of people who experienced, or claimed to experience, a state rather like the 'enlightenment' of the East.

For example, there was an heretical movement during the Middle Ages known as the Brethren of the Free Spirit:

> *The metaphysical framework was provided by Neo-Platonism; but all the efforts that had been made, from Pseudo-Dionysius and Erigena onwards, to adapt Neo-Platonism to Christian beliefs were discounted. The pantheism of Plotinus, so far from being slurred over, was emphasized. The Brethren of the Free Spirit did not hesitate to say: 'God is all that is', 'God is in every stone and in each limb of the human body as surely as in the Eucharistic bread', 'Every created thing is divine'. At the same time they took over Plotinus' own interpretation of this pantheism. It was the eternal essence of things, not their existence in time, that was truly God; whatever had a separate, transitory existence had emanated from God, but no longer was God. On the other hand whatever existed was bound to yearn for its Divine Origin and to strive to find its way back to that Origin;*

and at the end of time everything would, in fact, be reabsorbed in God. No emanation would remain, nothing would exist in separateness, there would no longer be anything capable of knowing, wishing, acting. All that would be left would be one single Essence, changeless, inactive; one all-embracing 'Blessedness'. Even the Persons of the Trinity, the Brethren of the Free Spirit insisted, would be submerged in that undifferentiated One. At the end of time, God really would be All.

Even now reabsorption was the fate of the human soul as soon as the body was dead. On the death of the body the soul disappeared into its Divine Origin like a drop of water which has been taken from a jug and then dropped back in again, or like a drop of wine in the sea. This doctrine amounted, of course, to an assurance of a universal, though impersonal, salvation; and the more consistent of the Brethren of the Free Spirit did, in fact, hold that heaven and hell were merely states of the soul in this world and that there was no after-life of punishment and reward . . . .

. . . Plotinus had held that human beings could even experience something of this reabsorption before the death of the body. It was possible for the soul to escape from its sensual bonds and from its awareness of itself and to sink for a moment, motionless and unconscious, into the One. This was the aspect of Neo-Platonism which appealed to the Brethren of the Free Spirit.

The Pursuit of the Millennium, Norman Cohn,
Pimlico, 1993

Absorption states

Normally people's minds are jumping around from one object to the next, but it is possible through practice to train your mind to concentrate. There is nothing bizarre or supernatural about this – it is simply a fact, an observation about how the mind works.

There is no essential difference between minds that are concentrated on playing the piano, building a wall or performing surgery, and

minds which are concentrated in contemplation or meditation. The thing or activity which is being concentrated on is different, but the minds are in a similar state to one another, namely that they are absorbed, relaxed and focused.

The great discovery of the East, also known but generally forgotten in the West, is that the concentrated mind can be made to become more and more concentrated and that, depending on the method used and the object of concentration, mental abilities appear which are not normally under conscious control.

If you haven't tried it then you won't be able to understand it, but many readers will have had enough experience to know what is meant. In India you hear a lot of talk about various kinds of *samadhi* or bliss states. Once you are a virtuoso at concentrating, it is possible to enter very, very deep states of concentration in which your body is still and you have no external awareness – you are totally absorbed in the object of your contemplation.

A great deal of interesting scientific research has been done on these unusual mental states using yogis and fakirs as experimental subjects. Some individuals are able to demonstrate the ability to consciously control their brainwaves, or to slow their heartbeats down to nothing, and this can be measured using conventional instruments.

From the point of view of the yogi, the object of the exercise is not simply to be able to slow your heartbeat down or to demonstrate some other trivial ability. To the yogi, it is his or her own experience that matters. In these deep states of absorption people report a variety of states of samadhi.

Before the Buddha achieved his Buddahood under the bodhi tree he trained for years with a number of different teachers. Among other things he learned to enter, he said, all the possible absorption states. None of them were satisfactory to him because they didn't give any final answer to the 'Who am I?' question.

Some people find it quite easy to enter samadhi states which can become addictive. You can get so attached to being in samadhi that you cling to it as strongly as other people cling to their money or

their lovers, or any mundane object of desire. If this happens you get stuck, and the enlightenment tradition says you have to give it up.

Here's a story to illustrate the problem.

An ascetic lived in isolation on a mountain for many years practising concentration until he finally managed to enter deep states of absorption. One day he went down from the mountain to a city. In the market place he was disturbed by all the hustle and bustle. Someone stepped on his foot and the pain made him angry. All his previous bliss and mental discipline had not removed his attachment to 'things' or left him completely free of ill will. There was still a 'little me' inside him to experience aversion and clinging.

In the enlightenment tradition, whether Buddhist or non-Buddhist, absorption states are not seen as the final answer to everything, but merely as a stage on the road. These are subtle things, which is why it is helpful to have a teacher who can give you personal guidance.

Here's an extract from a talk given by Acchaan Dhammadaru, a Thai monk, which describes how one may mistakenly think that one is experiencing ultimate emptiness. The extract uses English words in unusual ways because of the difficulty of translating Buddhist terminology, which illustrates the problem of language discussed earlier:

Sometimes when mindfulness and concentration are strong and the meditator departs from the four foundations of mindfulness, the mind is elevated and experiences void as if there is no self, both inside and outside. When this takes place, one may feel as if he is free from defilements. But clinging is still present in a dormant state in this voidness. Whenever this happens, the meditator should note that he has gone astray from the true path to nirvana and is going towards absorption. Note that the voidness of nirvana is quite different from absorption. Such a voidness is the outcome of meditation directed towards nirvana as an object. To experience this means cultivating continuous mindfulness. When the inner mind is seen, one will see it as a group or a cluster of many things. When insight develops further, one can perceive change each thought moment. Then one's sense of solidity or self is broken and the sense of emptiness of self is established. This destroys the myth of soul. The other

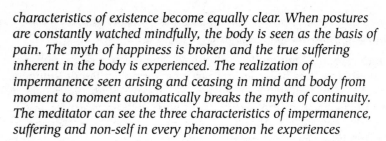

characteristics of existence become equally clear. When postures are constantly watched mindfully, the body is seen as the basis of pain. The myth of happiness is broken and the true suffering inherent in the body is experienced. The realization of impermanence seen arising and ceasing in mind and body from moment to moment automatically breaks the myth of continuity. The meditator can see the three characteristics of impermanence, suffering and non-self in every phenomenon he experiences

> *Living Buddhist Masters*, Jack Kornfield
> Unity Press, 1977

Here is a brief guide to the special meanings of some of the words in the above extract:

- 'Defilements' are desire, aversion and delusion about the true nature of things.
- 'Impermanence' is the idea that anything that comes into existence must one day cease to exist.
- 'Suffering' means the unsatisfactory experience of clinging to things that will one day cease to exist.
- 'Non-self' means 'big I'. It is the 'nothingness' which is not 'nothing', that cannot be described adequately in words but can only be experienced.

CRAZY WISDOM

There is a tradition of a certain path, suitable only for unusual people, called 'Crazy Wisdom'. In Crazy Wisdom you devote yourself to acting spontaneously, apparently without any discipline at all. Seeing the universe as a net of illusions, the seeker makes a special point of seeking out anything dangerous or horrible as a way of developing 'non-attachment'. As you might expect, Crazy Wisdom is said to be a dangerous path, especially dangerous if you do not remember to cultivate compassion and loving kindness on this path.

Charles Manson, the notorious leader of the 'Manson Family' whose followers committed the Sharon Tate murders in the 1960s, seems to

have discovered and practised certain aspects of Crazy Wisdom, but failed to cultivate loving kindness.

More recently, Stephen Seagal, the 43-year-old star of a number of violent films, has been declared to be a 'terton' by Penor Rinpoche, the Supreme Head of the Nyingma School of Tibetan Buddhism. A terton is someone who is capable of understanding the root teachings of Tibetan Buddhism. According to the Crazy Wisdom tradition, however bizarrely or immorally a terton may appear to be behaving, he (or she) may be a highly awake and evolved individual, the reincarnation, perhaps, of some high lama!

Big I is beyond rules.

May all beings be happy.

MAINTAINING
WELL-BEING

This chapter will give you some ideas on various matters which may help you to maintain a feeling of well-being:

- *diet*
- *ways of making a living*
- *posture.*

DIET

So much is said about diet these days that people are more confused than ever about what is the 'correct diet'. As in everything else, the important thing about your diet is for it to be balanced and realistic. Food and drink have a powerful effect on your states of mind, as well as on your health. The habits of eating that you acquire when you are young go deep, and we tend to associate different foods and ways of eating with pleasant or unpleasant memories. I always feel happy when I'm on the Mediterranean coast eating fresh produce and drinking a glass of wine, for instance – but I know people who feel uncomfortable and unhappy doing this.

The industrialisation of food production has given people much more choice, genuine as well as apparent, than anybody ever had in the past, but with this has come all kinds of problems. Anorexia and bulimia are modern diseases – as is widespread obesity. Almost everyone seems to suffer from bad eating habits of one kind or another.

Mystics have always paid attention to their diets, and many have stuck to extremely restricted diets for long periods of time. They do

this to get specific results, not because of religious or moral beliefs. By experimenting with your diet you can learn a great deal about who you are.

Some people believe that eating meat is wrong, or 'unspiritual', while others are against alcohol for similar reasons, yet Tibetan Buddhists eat meat because of the harsh climate (how many people know that the Dalai Lama is *not* a vegetarian?) and Jesus apparently drank wine, so why worry?

EXERCISE

Pick a mealtime which you know will be regular for the next three months – it doesn't matter which one it is – and resolve to practise the following discipline:

1 As you sit down to the meal, prepare yourself to pay close attention to exactly how you experience eating.

2 Don't read or talk. At this meal you are just going to concentrate on yourself eating.

3 Watch your feelings as you prepare to take the first morsel into your mouth – and see how they change when the food actually reaches your tongue.

4 Chew very slowly, and concentrate on how the food changes. 'Observe' it going down into your stomach.

5 Try to notice the difference in your reactions to different foods – if you like broccoli more than potatoes, for instance, really try to see how you feel about them as you eat them.

6 If there is a food which you don't like, pay particular attention to your reactions to it as you eat.

7 Try to be aware of how the food literally 'becomes' you during the digestive process.

This is a profound practice. The more you do it the more you will learn. At first it will be difficult to do it if you are eating with other people who don't know what you are up to (and it is generally better not to tell them), so make sure you pick a meal where you are not going to be disturbed, even if it is only a private snack before bedtime.

Ways of making a living

Some ways of making a living do much more harm than good; the obvious ones are:

- the arms industry
- robbery
- drug dealing.

Here are some that are less obvious:

- high-pressure selling of bad products to people who can't afford them
- selling products and services that make people ill
- promising people things that you know will never happen
- cheating the weak.

Ethical issues of this kind crop up in all forms of work, but deliberately harmful behaviour is institutionalised in many organisations, including companies, the professions and government departments. It is hard to say 'no' to a boss when your job is on the line, everyone else is doing the same thing and there is a whole set of convincing justifications for doing what you know, secretly, is harmful to others.

An extreme example of this is the nazification of Germany in the 1930s. Ordinary people found it extremely hard not to go along with what was happening in every walk of life, even if they knew they didn't like it.

If you find yourself being asked to do something which you sincerely feel is harmful in the course of your job, and you are not allowed to refuse, then perhaps it is time to look for another job. Jobs that make you hate yourself aren't worth doing.

Posture

The way you stand and walk reveals an enormous amount to the trained eye about your personality. What is your normal posture?

Do you slouch? Do you force your shoulders back tensely? When you sit, is your back straight?

The mind and the body are intimately related. Our habits of mind are reflected in the habitual postures that we allow our body to hold. By changing bodily postures we can actually change our habits of mind. It really works!

Traditionally, a balanced posture is one where the back is vertically straight, or, if you are lying down, horizontally straight and symmetrical. This doesn't mean that you have to hold your body rigidly in place. Sitting straight and standing straight may feel strange at first if you are not used to it, but in time it will seem the most natural thing in the world.

Conclusion

I hope that this book has helped to give you a sense of what the enlightenment tradition is all about. It can be summed up in these three sentences:

- Be here now.
- Maintain a warm heart to all beings.
- Stop clinging.

May all beings be happy.

10

THE LIFE OF
THE BUDDHA

The story of Siddhartha Gautama, the historical Buddha, has come down to us from records written some centuries after his death on or about 483 BC. We can be as confident that he really existed as we can be about many other figures, such as Jesus Christ or Zoroaster, of whom no contemporary records survive. Like many other founders of religious organisations, the Buddha's life is surrounded by legend, and it is not always easy to distinguish between an actual report of events and later pious embellishments. As with all leaders there was inevitably a political dimension to the Buddha's work, and as his followers increased, he evidently had to deal with secular authorities and hostile belief systems.

The purpose of this chapter is simply to retell the basic story of the Buddha's life and to put it into context. People who are new to oriental philosophy sometimes have the impression that his life and teachings were unique, but in fact his career follows the tradition of the Indian holy man that was ancient even in his time. That he discovered the 'ultimate truth' of reality, as, perhaps, have not so very many others, is for every individual to decide for themselves. To say that only a Buddha can recognise another Buddha may be true, but is a circular argument. We who are not Buddhas are being told of a state of being which we cannot understand because we do not experience it – how can a practical person swallow this? The traditional answer is that 'we' are all Buddhas; inside us there is an essential 'Buddha nature' which we can find for ourselves, if we wish to look for it.

Early Life and Influences

Siddhartha Gautama was born to a prince of the Gautama clan of the Sakya tribe, south of the Himalayas in what is now Nepal. He is said to have been brought up in secluded luxury in a palace, surrounded by wives and concubines and following the life of a spoilt warrior princeling. It is said that his father, Suddhodana, had sought to protect him from knowledge of the sorrows of the world, and had prevented him from being exposed to suffering and religious contact in order to train him for his princely role.

When he was about twenty-nine years old, Siddhartha encountered an old man for the first time in his life. He was shocked to see his decrepitude. Later he happened to see a sick person and learned about the loathsome nature of disease, and not long after he witnessed a corpse at a funeral. These events are said to have stunned Siddhartha into wondering about the meaning of life and the reason for its shortness.

Search for the Meaning of Life

For many thousands of years Indians have accepted that some people need to give up their responsibilities to concentrate on their inner life. Like many hot countries, India is a noisy, dirty place where everybody pokes their noses into other people's business; the only way to get peace and quiet is to go off and be on your own, away from human habitation. Traditionally such 'renunciates' have lived by begging for a bare minimum of food, and lay people have supplied them, sometimes reluctantly, with the basic necessities of life.

To get to the bottom of his difficulties, Siddhartha had to get away from the palace, and when he met one of the wandering holy men (*sadhus*) who are still to be found throughout India, the answer was clear: having had a son, the royal succession was established, so he gave up his princely robes and wandered south to seek the company of sadhus.

Siddhartha became the student of a sage named Alara Kalama and practised yoga and meditation. Evidently he had a great deal of natural ability, for he rapidly mastered the techniques and was able to reach high states of meditation. Finding this unsatisfactory, he then went to another teacher, Uddaka Ramaputra, and attained an even higher state of consciousness.

These high states still did not provide Siddhartha with the answers he sought, and he decided to follow another ancient sadhu tradition – that of extreme austerity. He practised breathing and other yogic techniques with great intensity for long periods. Then he decided to try starvation. Sitting in meditation, accompanied by a few disciples, Siddhartha took no food until his flesh wasted away and his bones showed clearly through his skin.

After six years of severe privation, Siddhartha decided it was pointless to go on; he decided that these activities were neither better nor worse than living a life of ease and luxury. He started eating again. The disciples who were with him were horrified and left him, saying that he strayed from the path of holiness.

ENLIGHTENMENT

Regaining his strength Siddartha started to meditate successfully again, and went through many states in which he was able to observe, with his inner eye, much about the origin and phenomena of creation. He sat beneath a tree at Bodhgaya, in what is now the State of Bihar in India, and vowed that he wouldn't move until he attained enlightenment. As described in the Buddhist scriptures, Siddhartha went through a series of states, each shedding light on the nature of things, and cleansed himself of the remaining impurities, symbolised as the demon *Mara* with whom he is said to have battled.

The conclusions that Siddhartha came to during this time under the tree were in essence, that all things are subject to birth, growth and death and that 'clinging' to things causes suffering; the personality

and even the mind are transitory phenomena as are all other things and the true nature of reality is a vast emptiness.

According to legend, when Siddhartha had this realisation, he touched the ground, calling on the earth to witness his release from the eternal round of birth, life and death, and the earth swayed like a drunken woman and flowers rained from the sky.

When morning came, Siddhartha looked upon the world with new eyes. He was now *Buddha*, the 'One who is awake' and the *Tathagata*, which means 'thus gone' or 'thus come'. Sitting for some time under the tree, he began to reflect on how he might tell others about his discoveries. At first it seemed to him that there was little point in attempting to do so, since people are so strongly attached to notions about their existence that the Buddha could now see were illusory. Later, he reflected that there were some people who had 'only a little dust in their eyes' who could be taught and, it is said, out of compassion for humanity's suffering, he decided to do so.

The Buddha walked to the holy city of Benares and found the companions who had been with him during his years of asceticism. They still criticized him for living in abundance, but the Buddha explained that he did not live in abundance and that the extremes are not to be practised by the one who is enlightened – neither the life of passions and luxury, nor the life of self-torture. Avoiding these two extremes, the enlightened follow the middle path which produces insight and knowledge and leads to peace, wisdom, enlightenment, and *nirvana*.

ḣis ɒoctrine

Buddha then expounded the four 'Noble Truths' of his doctrine.

The first Noble Truth relates to what is normally translated as 'suffering' or 'pain', but it is perhaps more correctly understood as the unsatisfactory nature of things: we may be happy for a time, but there is something unsatisfactory about it because it cannot last forever, and when we are unhappy this is also unsatisfactory.

The second Noble Truth relates to the cause of this unsatisfactory state of affairs, which, said the Buddha, comes from a craving to 'be' something, to have desires and aversions and to believe that one is a permanent entity.

The third Noble Truth is how this unsatisfactory condition can cease, simply by abandoning mental attachment to anything, including our own sense of being a creature separate from the rest of the world.

The fourth Noble Truth is how to conduct oneself to abandon such attachments, which is by the famous Buddhist 'Eightfold Path', a prescription for living categorised as correct understanding, correct intention, correct speech, correct action, correct livelihood, correct attention, correct concentration, and correct meditation.

His former companions were converted by his teachings, and followed him as he wandered around northern India, practising meditation and begging for alms. Gradually other people were attracted to him and a Buddhist community, known as the *sangha*, grew up, consisting of monks, who renounced normal life and lived on alms, and lay people, who practised the Buddha's teachings (*Dharma*) while continuing to live as householders.

CONTEMPORARY TEAChING

Northern India was plainly in a period of much intellectual ferment at the time of the Buddha. Holy men taught a whole range of philosophies and mystical paths ranging from the extremes of atheism and scepticism to spirit worship and idolatry. *Brahmanism*, the priestly cult of high-caste Hindus, was apparently already showing signs of its tendency towards elitism and the exclusion of non-Brahmans, and the Buddha tangled with it many times, arguing that the supreme God of Brahmanism – *Brahma* – was an entity subject to birth and death like all others. In contrast to the Brahmans, the Buddha made a point of teaching in the common language of the time and would accept anyone as a follower, regardless of their social background.

One of the other holy men living in the same part of India at the same time as the Buddha also started a movement that has survived until today. His name was *Mahavir*, the founder of *Jainism*. Curiously, many of the epithets used for the Buddha are also used of Mahavir (which means 'Great Man').

The Buddha lived until about the age of eighty, teaching and meditating. The Buddhist scriptures report many of his encounters with all kinds of people; he talked with kings as well as with the common people and dealt with every possible problem and difficulty with regard to the Dharma. It has been remarked that the repetitive nature of these scriptures may possibly be an accurate record – like many good teachers, the Buddha may have had set, formal speeches which he would repeat word for word at mass meetings, often to an unconverted audience. What is clear, though, is that he spent much of the time sitting in silence: he was not an evangelist who spent all his time glad-handing the public and giving rousing addresses.

Tales about the Buddha

There is not enough space here to repeat every tale told of the Buddha, but here are a few that may be of interest.

In the ninth year after the enlightenment, the Buddha was at Kaushambi, and the monk Malunkyaputra complained that the Buddha never explained whether the world is eternal or temporary, finite or infinite, or whether life and the body are the same or different, or whether *arhats* (enlightened beings) are beyond death or not. He even threatened to leave the Community if the Buddha would not answer his questions.

First the Buddha asked him if he had ever promised to explain these things; the monk agreed that he had not. Then he told the story of a man who was pierced by a poisoned arrow, and his relatives summoned a doctor. Suppose, he said, the physician had said that he would not remove the arrow nor treat the patient until his questions had been answered, such as who made the bow, what kind it was, all about the arrow, and so on. The man would die, and still the information would not be known. Then the Buddha told

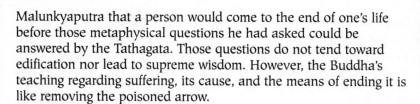

Malunkyaputra that a person would come to the end of one's life before those metaphysical questions he had asked could be answered by the Tathagata. Those questions do not tend toward edification nor lead to supreme wisdom. However, the Buddha's teaching regarding suffering, its cause, and the means of ending it is like removing the poisoned arrow.

The Buddha remained silent or enigmatic on many metaphysical issues; he did not provide a ready-made, all-encompassing cosmology for others to believe in. Sometimes he spoke in terms of entities and religious ideas that were common in his time without necessarily believing in them himself, to establish a basis for communication. We can understand this as 'seeing where the other person is coming from'. For example, if you want to communicate with someone who is terrified of ghosts, you may get further by talking about ghosts as if they exist than if you keep telling the person that ghosts aren't real.

The Buddha addressed a group of people called the Kalamas, who were confused by all the conflicting claims of the different religious systems. Buddha advised them to verify all claims themselves by examining which doctrines lead to positive results, and which lead to negative ones. The former should be adopted, and the latter rejected:

> 'Do not be [convinced] by reports, tradition, or hearsay; nor by skill in the scriptural collections, argumentation, or reasoning; nor after examining conditions or considering theories; nor because [a theory] fits appearances, nor because of respect for an ascetic [who holds a particular view]. Rather, Kalamas, when you know for yourselves: these doctrines are non-virtuous; these doctrines are erroneous; these doctrines are rejected by the wise, these doctrines, when performed and undertaken, lead to loss and suffering – then you should reject them, Kalamas.'

By their fruits ye shall know them – you can be fooled in the short term by strong claims and good arguments, but time will reveal the effects of any practice or belief. The Buddha tried starvation, for example, before rejecting it as useless.

Nirvana, or *nibbana* as it is known in Pali, the language of the early Buddhist scriptures, is one of those words that everybody knows and nobody understands (a bit like 'democracy', maybe!). Nirvana is said to be the final cessation of suffering, a state beyond the cycle of birth and death. As such, it could be said to be the ultimate goal of the path taught by the Buddha. There are only a few descriptions of nirvana in Buddhist literature:

> 'Monks, there is that sphere in which there is neither earth nor water, fire nor air: it is not the infinity of space, nor the infinity of perception; it is not nothingness, nor is it either idea or non-idea; it is neither this world nor the next, nor is it both; it is neither the sun nor the moon.

> Monks, I declare that it neither comes nor goes, it neither abides nor passes away; it is not caused, established, begun, supported: it is the end of suffering.

> What I call the selfless is hard to see, for it is not easy to see the truth. But he who knows it penetrates his craving; and for him who sees it, there is nothing there.

> Monks, there is an unborn, unbecome, unmade, unconditioned. Monks, if there were not an unborn, unbecome, unmade, unconditioned, then we could not here know any escape from the born, become, made, conditioned...

> For the attached there is wandering, but for the unattached there is no wandering: without wandering there is serenity; when there is serenity there is no lust; without lust there is neither coming nor going; without coming or going there is neither passing away nor being reborn; without passing away or being reborn there is neither this life nor the next, nor anything between them. It is the end of suffering.'

Still confused? Don't worry. If it is real you have as much of it as anyone else. Worrying about nirvana is just about the most useless activity devised by man, and is not central to the objects of the Buddha Dharma.

Ðᴇᴘᴇɴᴅᴇɴᴛ Aʀɪꜱɪɴɢ

'Dependent Arising' is an important idea of the Buddha's. After attaining awakening, the Buddha indicated that he had come to realize that all the phenomena of the universe are interconnected by relationships of mutual causality. Things come into being in dependence upon causes and conditions, abide due to causes and conditions, and eventually pass away due to causes and conditions. Thus, the world is viewed by Buddhists as a dynamic and ever-changing system. Because of a basic misunderstanding of the workings of reality (referred to as 'ignorance'), people falsely imagine that some worldly things can bring them happiness, and thus they generate desire and try to acquire these things. Such attitudes provide the basis for the arising of negative mental states, and these states in turn lead to other negative effects, including the birth of other beings in the future.

This can be confusing – did the Buddha mean that most of us are doomed to perpetual reincarnation, as so many people think? The following story sheds light on what he meant:

Once a certain monk conceived the following wrong view:

> 'As I understand the Bhagavan's (Blessed One) doctrine, this consciousness continues on, moves on [throughout transmigration], and not another [consciousness].'

In other words, the monk was saying that he thought that his consciousness – or soul – would enter other bodies in the future.

The Buddha summoned him and after hearing what he had to say, reproved him:

> 'Whom do you tell, you foolish person, that I have taught such a doctrine? Haven't I said, with many similes, that consciousness is not independent, but comes about through the chain of Dependent Arising and can never arise without a cause? You foolish person, you misunderstand and misrepresent me, and so you undermine your own position and produce much demerit. You bring upon yourself lasting harm and sorrow!...'

Then the Bhagavan addressed the assembled monks, saying:

> 'Whatever form of consciousness arises from a condition is
> known by the name of that condition; thus, if it arises from the
> eye and from forms it is known as visual consciousness . . .
> and so with the senses of hearing, smell, taste, touch, and
> mind, and their objects. It's just like a fire, which you call by
> the name of the fuel: a wood fire, a fire of sticks, a grass fire, a
> cow-dung fire, a fire of husks, a rubbish fire, and so on . . .
> In the same way, monks, when due to an appropriate condition
> a consciousness arises, it is known by this or that name . . .'

Do you get it? From the Buddha's point of view, what we think as
our consciousness is itself a concatenation of ever-changing forces,
dependent upon other things – there is thus no permanent 'soul' to
move on to another body. This idea disturbs a lot of people in the
West because it seems very negative and fatalistic, but the beauty of
the Buddha Dharma is that it offers ways of checking the truth out
for yourself. By checking it out, you can come to see that, awesome
and terrifying though it is to experience, even soul and
consciousness are temporary things.

Final years

When he reached the age of eighty, the Tathagata's body seemed to
lessen in vitality, and he declared that he had only three months to
live. His companion Ananda missed the chance to beg him to stay
until the end of the aeon as Buddhas can do, according to legend.

The Buddha ate a meal provided by a smith; it is not exactly clear
what it contained, but it may have been mushrooms. Violent
sickness followed, with a flow of blood and deadly pains, but the
Buddha mindfully controlled them and declared that he would die in
the third watch of the night. After giving some instruction and being
visited by followers, he said, 'Everything that is born is subject to
decay. It is up to each of you to work out your own liberation with
diligence,' and died.

The death and rebirth of Buddhism

The subsequent history of Buddhism is long and interesting. As with other movements, over time it split into various groups and sects, some of which appeared to disagree on many matters. Eventually Buddhism died out in India – by 1300 AD it had vanished, finished off by the Islamic invasions – but it had already manifested in new, vigorous forms in Sri Lanka, China, Tibet, Japan and elsewhere. The diversity and richness of Buddhist culture is staggering, but there is no need for a Westerner to feel left out, or unable to understand it; the Buddha was not a mystifier, even if what he says may sometimes seem mysterious. You are just as important as anyone else and you have an equal opportunity to examine your true, original and universal nature.

Be here now.

fURTDER READING

The following books helped me in the writing of this one. They will not, of course, give you the experience of enlightenment – only you can do that!

Alpert, Richard (Baba Ram Dass), *Be Here Now*, Lama Foundation, 1971

Blackmore, Sue, *Dying to Live*, Heinemann, 1992

Brunton, Paul, *A Search in Secret India*, Rider, 1913

Brunton, Paul, *A Search in Secret Egypt*, Rider, 1936

Cohn, Norman, *The Pursuit of the Millennium*, Pimlico, 1993

Dass, Ram with Levine, Stephen, *Grist for the Mill*, Unity Press, 1971

Huxley, Aldous, *Island*, Perennial Classic, 1972

Isherwood, Christopher, *My Guru and His Disciple*, HarperCollins, 1968

James, William, *The Varieties of Religious Experience*, Longman, 1902

Kornfield, Jack, *Living Buddhist Masters*, Unity Press, 1977

Nyanamoli, Bhikku, *The Life of the Buddha*, Buddhist Publication Society, Kandy, 1971

Page, Tim, *Page After Page*, Sidgwick & Jackson, 1988

Ramana, Maharshi, *Talks, Ramanaramam*, Tiruvannamalai, S. India, 1958

St. John of the Cross, *The Dark Night of the Soul*, trans. E. Allison Peers, Image Books, New York, 1959

Walshe, Maurice (Transl.), *Thus Have I Heard, The Long Discourses of the Buddha*, Wisdom Publications, 1987

Yates, Frances, *The Art of Memory*, RKP, 1966

Yates, Frances, *Giordano Bruno and the Hermetic Tradition*, University of Chicago Press, 1964

The following list gives Douglas Harding's work that is currently in print:

Harding, D.E., *The Little Book of Life and Death*, Arkana 1988

Harding, D.E., *On Having No Head; Zen and the Re-discovery of the Obvious*, Penguin Arkana, 1986

Harding, D.E., *The Science of the First Person: Its Principles, Practice and Potential*, Shollond Trust, Ipswich, IP10 OEW, 1997

Harding, D.E., *The Hierarchy of Heaven and Earth*, Florida University, 1979

Harding, D.E., *Look For Yourself*, Shollond Trust, Ipswich, 1996

Harding, D.E., *Religions of the World*, Shollond Trust, Ipswich, 1995

Harding, D.E., *The Spectre in the Lake*, Shollond Trust, Ipswich, 1996

Periodicals:

The Headless Way, Ed. Richard Lang, 87b Cazenove Road, London N16 BB, tel. 0181 806 3710

Vivre sans tête, 58 Rue de la Marne, N10RT France 79000

useful addresses

Most of the addresses given are of places that teach *Vipassana*, or 'Insight Meditation', which was taught by the Buddha. It really works. It has absolutely nothing to do with your religious or philosophical beliefs, so don't worry about being brain-washed – in fact, if you practise well, the opposite tends to happen!

United Kingdom and Europe
Douglas Harding
Sholland House
Nacton
Ipswich
IP10 0EW
Tel: 01473 659558

Satyananda Yoga Centre
70 Thurleigh Road
London
SW1 2UD
Tel: 0171 673 4869

Vipassana Meditation Centre
Dhamma Dipa
Harewood End
Hereford
HR2 8JS
Tel: 01989 730234

Centre Vipassana France
'Le Bois Plante'
Louesme
89350 Champignelles
France
Tel: (33) 386 45-75-14

Vipassana Meditationshaus
Kirchenweg 2
76332
Bad Herrenalb
Germany
Tel: (49) 07083 51169

Scandinavian School of Yoga
Haa Course Centre
340 13 Hamneda
Sweden
Tel: (46) 372 55063

United States
California Vipassana Center
PO Box 1167
North Fork
Calif. 93643
Tel: (209) 877-4386

Australia and New Zealand
Vipassana Meditation Centre
PO Box 103
Blackheath
NSW 2785
Australia
Tel: (61) 047 877 436

Vipassana Centre Queensland
Dhamma Rasmi
PO Box 119
Rules Road
Pomona
Queensland 4568
Australia
Tel: (61) 07 485 2452

India and the East
Nilambe Meditation Centre
Nilambe
Sri Lanka

Mahabodhi International
  Meditation Centre
Devachan
PO Box 22
Leh
194101
Ladakh
Tel: (91) 80 225 0684

Vipassana Meditation Center
PO Box 24
Shelburne Falls
Mass. 01370
Tel: (413) 625 2160

Vipassana Centre
Burnside Road
RD 3
Kaukapakapa
New Zealand
Tel: (64) 09 420 5319

Te Moata Meditation Centre
PO Box 100
Tairua
New Zealand
64 7868 8798

Wat Thai Monastery
Bodh Gaya
Bihar
India

Annual Bodh Gaya Retreat, India

Bodh Gaya is the place in India where Siddhartha Gautama became the Buddha, and is now a pilgrimage centre. Christopher Titmuss, a former Buddhist monk, holds a 10-day retreat there on the same dates every year at a Thai monastery a few minutes' walk from the Bodhi Tree, a descendant of the original tree under which the Buddha sat. The retreats are held in silence except for personal meetings with the teachers, small group meetings and inquiry sessions in the meditation hall. The practice of Vipassana meditation includes sitting, walking, standing, reclining and eating. Two substantial meals are served each day. Smoking is not permitted and people stay for the full duration of the retreat within the grounds of the monastery.

The cost is approximately $7 a day, to cover food, accommodation and other expenses. The dates are:

7–17 January
17–27 January
28 January–4 February

For further information or to register for a retreat, contact:

BEFORE 1 NOVEMBER
Gaia House
West Ogwell
Near Newton Abbott
Devon
TQ12 6EN
Tel. 01626 333613
e-mail: gaiahouse@gn.apc.org

AFTER 1 NOVEMBER
Thomas Jost
c/o Postmaster
Bodh Gaya
District Gaya
Bihar 824231
India

OTHER TITLES IN THIS SERIES

Astral Projection 0 340 67418 0   £5.99   Is it possible for the soul to leave the body at will? In this book the traditional techniques used to achieve astral projection are described in a simple, practical way, and Out of the Body and Near Death Experiences are also explored.

Chakras 0 340 62082 X   £5.99   The body's energy centres, the chakras, can act as gateways to healing and increased self-knowledge. This book shows you how to work with chakras in safety and with confidence.

Chinese Horoscopes 0 340 64804 X   £5.99   In the Chinese system of horoscopes, the year of birth is all-important. *Chinese Horoscopes for beginners* tells you how to determine your own Chinese horoscope, what personality traits you are likely to have, and how your fortunes may fluctuate in years to come.

Dowsing 0 340 60882 X   £5.99   People all over the world have used dowsing since the earliest times. This book shows how to start dowsing – what to use, what to dowse, and what to expect when subtle energies are detected.

Dream Interpretation 0 340 60150 7   £5.99   This fascinating introduction to the art and science of dream interpretation explains how to unravel the meaning behind dream images to interpret your own and other people's dreams.

Feng Shui 0 340 62079 X   £5.99   This beginner's guide to the ancient art of luck management will show you how to increase your good fortune and well-being by harmonising your environment with the natural energies of the earth.

Gems and Crystals 0 340 60883 8   £5.99   For centuries gems and crystals have been used as an aid to healing and meditation. This guide tells you all you need to know about choosing, keeping and using stones to increase your personal awareness and improve your well-being.

The Goddess 0 340 68390 2   £5.99   This book traces the development, demise and rebirth of the Goddess, looking at the worship of Her and retelling myths from all over the world.

Graphology 0 340 60625 8   £5.99   Graphology, the science of interpreting handwriting to reveal personality, is now widely accepted and used throughout the world. This introduction will enable you to make a comprehensive analysis of your own and other people's handwriting to reveal the hidden self.

Herbs for Magic and Ritual 0 340 67415 6   £4.99   This book looks at the well-known herbs and the stories attached to them. There is information on the use of herbs in essential oils and incense, and on their healing and magical qualities.

I Ching 0 340 62080 3   £5.99   The roots of *I Ching* or the *Book of Changes* lie in the time of the feudal mandarin lords of China, but its traditional wisdom is still relevant today. Using the original poetry in its translated form, this introduction traces its history, survival and modern-day applications.

Interpreting Signs and Symbols 0 340 68827 0   £5.99   The history of signs and symbols is traced in this book from their roots to the modern age. It also examines the way psychiatry uses symbolism, and the significance of doodles.

The Language of Flowers 0 340 69781 4 £5.99 Flowers can heal us both emotionally and physically. Find out how, and learn about superstitions associated with flowers and how to enhance your life with flowers, in this book.

Love Signs 0 340 64805 8 £5.99 This is a practical introduction to the astrology of romantic relationships. It explains the different roles played by each of the planets, focusing particularly on the position of the Moon at the time of birth.

Meditation 0 340 64835 X £5.99 This beginner's guide gives simple, clear instructions to enable you to start meditating and benefiting from this ancient mental discipline immediately. The text is illustrated throughout by full-colour photographs and line drawings.

Mediumship 0 340 68009 1 £5.99 Whether you want to become a medium yourself, or simply understand what mediumship is about, this book will give you the grounding to undertake a journey of discovery into the spirit realms.

The Moon and You 0 340 64836 8 £5.99 The phase of the Moon when you were born radically affects your personality. This book looks at nine lunar types – how they live, love, work and play, and provides simple tables to find out the phase of your birth.

Numerology 0 340 59551 5 £5.99 Despite being scientifically based, numerology requires no great mathematical talents to understand. This introduction gives you all the information you will need to understand the significance of numbers in your everyday life.

Pagan Gods for Today's Man 0 340 69130 1 £5.99 Looking at ancient gods and old stories, this guide explores the social and psychological issues affecting the role of men today. In these pages men of all ages and persuasions can find inspiration.

Paganism 0 340 67013 4 £5.99 Pagans are true Nature worshippers who celebrate the cycles of life. This guide describes pagan festivals and rituals and takes a detailed look at the many forms of paganism practised today.

Palmistry 0 340 59552 3 £5.99 Palmistry is the oldest form of character reading still in use. This illustrated guide shows you exactly what to look for and how to interpret what you find.

Qabalah 0 340 67339 7 £5.99 The Qabalah is an ancient Jewish system of spiritual knowledge centred on the Tree of Life. This guide explains how it can be used in meditation and visualisation, and links it to the chakras, yoga, colour therapy, crystals, Tarot and numerology.

Runes 0 340 62081 1 £5.99 The power of the runes in healing and giving advice about relationships and life in general has been acknowledged since the time of the Vikings. This book shows how runes can be used in our technological age to increase personal awareness and stimulate individual growth.

Shamanism 0 340 68010 5 £5.99 Shamanic technique offers direct contact with Spirit, vivid self-knowledge and true kinship with plants, animals and the planet Earth. This book describes the shamanic way, the wisdom of the Medicine Wheel and power animals.

Spiritual Healing 0 340 67416 4   £5.99   All healing starts with self, and the Universal Power which makes this possible is available to everyone. In this book there are exercises, techniques and guidelines to follow which will enable you to heal yourself and others spiritually.

Star Signs 0 340 59553 1   £5.99   This detailed analysis looks at each of the star signs in turn and reveals how your star sign affects everything about you. This book shows you how to use this knowledge in your relationships and in everyday life.

Tantric Sexuality 0 340 68349 X   £5.99   Tantric Buddhists use sex as a pleasurable path to enlightenment. This guide offers a radically different and exciting new dimension to sex, explaining practical techniques in a clear and simple way.

Tarot 0 340 59550 7   £5.99   Tarot cards have been used for many centuries. This guide gives advice on which sort to buy, where to get them and how to use them. The emphasis is on using the cards positively, as a tool for gaining self-knowledge, while exploring present and future possibilities.

Visualisation 0 340 65495 3   £5.99   This introduction to visualisation, a form of self-hypnosis widely used by Buddhists, will show you how to practise the basic techniques – to relieve stress, improve your health and increase your sense of personal well-being.

Witchcraft 0 340 67014 2   £5.99   This guide to the ancient religion based on Nature worship answers many of the questions and uncovers the myths and misconceptions surrounding witchcraft. Mystical rituals and magic are explained and there is advice for the beginner on how to celebrate the Sabbats.

Working With Colour 0 340 67011 8   £5.99   Colour is the medicine of the future. This book explores the energy of each colour and its significance, gives advice on how colour can enhance our well-being, and gives ideas on using colour in the home and garden.

Your Psychic Powers 0 340 67417 2   £5.99   Are you psychic? This book will help you find out by encouraging you to look more deeply within yourself. Psychic phenomena such as precognitive dreams, out of body travels and visits from the dead are also discussed in this ideal stepping stone towards a more aware you.

To order this series

All books in this series are available from bookshops or, in case of difficulty, can be ordered direct from the publisher. Prices and availability subject to change without notice. Send your order with your name and address to : Hodder & Stoughton Ltd, Cash Sales Department, Bookpoint, 39 Milton Park, Abingdon, OXON, OX14 4TD, UK. If you have a credit card you may order by telephone – 01235 831700.

Please enclose a cheque or postal order made payable to Bookpoint Ltd, allow the following for postage and packing: UK & BFPO: £1.00 for the first book, 50p for the second book and 30p for each additional book ordered up to a maximum charge of £3.00. OVERSEAS & EIRE: £2.00 for the first book, £1.00 for the second book and 50p for each additional book.

For sales in the following countries please contact:

UNITED STATES: Trafalgar Square (Vermont), Tel: 800 423 4525 (toll-free)
CANADA: General Publishing (Ontario), Tel: 445 3333
AUSTRALIA: Hodder & Stoughton (Sydney), Tel: 02 638 5299